Bibliographies for Biblical Research

New Testament Series
in Twenty-One Volumes

General Editor

Watson E. Mills

Bibliographies for Biblical Research

New Testament Series
in Twenty-One Volumes

Volume XI

Philippians

Compiled by

Watson E. Mills

MELLEN BIBLICAL PRESS
Lewiston/Queenston/Lampeter

Library of Congress Cataloging-in-Publication Data

Bibliographies for biblical research.

    Includes index.
    Contents: v. 1. The Gospel of Matthew / compiled by
Watson E. Mills --   -- v. 11. Philippians
      1. Bible. N.T.--Criticism, interpretation, etc.--
Bibliography. I. Mills, Watson E.

Z7772.L1B4 1993 [BS2341.2]   016.2262'06   93-30864

ISBN 0-7734-2347-8 (v. 1) Matthew	ISBN 0-7734-2349-4 (v. 2) Mark
ISBN 0-7734-2385-0 (v. 3) Luke	ISBN 0-7734-2357-5 (v. 4) John
ISBN 0-7734-2432-6 (v. 5) Acts	ISBN 0-7734-2418-0 (v. 6) Romans
ISBN 0-7734-2419-9 (v. 7) 1 Corinthians	ISBN 0-7734-2442-3 (v. 8) 2 Corinthians
ISBN 0-7734-2468-7 (v. 9) Galatians	ISBN 0-7734-2472-5 (v. 10) Ephesians
ISBN 0-7734-2474-1 (v. 11) Philippians	ISBN 0-7734-2438-5 (v. 21) Revelation

This is volume 11 in the continuing series
Bibliographies for Biblical Research
New Testament Series
Volume 11 ISBN 0-7734-2474-1
Series ISBN 0-7734-9345-X

A CIP catalog record for this book is available from the British Library.

Copyright © 1999 The Edwin Mellen Press

The Edwin Mellen Press
Box 450
Lewiston, New York
USA 14092

The Edwin Mellen Press
Box 67
Queenston, Ontario
CANADA L0S 1L0

Edwin Mellen Press, Ltd.
Lampeter, Dyfed, Wales
UNITED KINGDOM SA48 7DY

Printed in the United States of America

Dedication

In memory of my grandfather

James Early Mills

1874-1954

with great affection

Contents

Introduction to the Series

This volume is the eleventh in a series of bibliographies on the books of the Hebrew and Christian Bibles as well as the deutero-canonicals. This ambitious series calls for some 35-40 volumes over the next 3-5 years compiled by practicing scholars from various traditions.

Each author (compiler) of these volumes is working within the general framework adopted for the series, i.e., citations are to works published within the twentieth century that make important contributions to the understanding of the text and backgrounds of the various books.

Obviously the former criterion is more easily quantifiable than the latter, and it is precisely at this point that an individual compiler makes her/his specific contribution. We are not intending to be comprehensive in the sense of definitive, but where resources are available, as many listings as possible have been included.

The arrangement for the entries, in most volumes in the series, consists of three divisions: scriptural citations; subject citations; commentaries. In some cases the first two categories may duplicate each other to some degree. Multiple citations by scriptural citation are also included where relevant.

Those who utilize these volumes are invited to assist the compilers by noting textual errors as well as obvious omissions that ought to be taken into account in subsequent printings. Perfection is nowhere more elusive than in the citation of bibliographic materials. We would welcome your assistance at this point.

When the series is completed, the entire contents of all volumes (updated) will be available on CD-ROM. This option will be available, without charge, to those who have subscribed to the casebound volumes.

We hope that these bibliographies will contribute to the discussions and research going on in the field among faculty as well as students. They should serve a significant role as reference works in both research and public libraries.

I wish to thank the staff and editors of the Edwin Mellen Press, and especially Professor Herbert Richardson, for the gracious support of this series.

Watson E. Mills, Series Editor
Mercer University
Macon GA 31211
November 1999

Preface

This Bibliography on the Epistle to the Philippians provides an index to the journal articles, essays in collected works, books and monographs and commentaries published in the twentieth century through the early months of 1999. Technical works of scholarship, from many differing traditions constitute the bulk of the citations though I have included some selected works that intend to reinterpret this research to a wider audience.

I acknowledge the work of Paul-Émile Langevin, *Bibliographie biblique* (Les Presses de l'Université Laval, 1972, 1978, 1985). This work is especially useful in verifying Catholic publications particularly citations to French literature. These volumes are meticulously indexed by scriptural citation as well as subject. Building the database necessary for a work of this magnitude was a tedious and time-consuming task. I acknowledge with gratitude the Education Commission of the Southern Baptist Convention which provided funds for travel to overseas libraries during the summers of 1994 and 1995, as well as Mercer University which also funded some of the travel costs.

I want to express my gratitude to the staff librarians at the following institutions: Baptist Theological Seminary (Rüschlikon, Switzerland); Oxford

University   (Oxford, UK); Emory University (Atlanta, GA); Duke University
(Durham, NC); University of Zürich (Zürich, Switzerland); Southern Baptist
Theological Seminary (Louisville, KY).

Watson E. Mills
Mercer University
Macon GA 31207
November 1999

Abbreviations

ABQ	*American Baptist Quarterly* (Valley Forge PA)
AJBI	*Annual of the Japanese Biblical Institute* (Tokyo)
AmCl	*L'Ami du Clerge* (Langres)
AsSeign	*Assemblees du Seigneur* (Paris)
AUSS	*Andrews University Seminary Studies* (Berrien Springs MI)
BI	*Biblical Illustrator* (Nashville TN)
Bib	*Biblica* (Rome)
BibN	*Biblische Notizen: Beiträge zur exegetischen Diskussion* (Bamberg)
BibO	*Bibbia e Oriente* (Milan)
BK	*Bibel und Kirche* (Stuttgart)
BL	*Bibel und Liturgie* (Vienna)
BSac	*Bibliotheca Sacra* (Dallas TX)
BTB	*Biblical Theology Bulletin* (Jamaica NY)
BVC	*Bible et Vie Chretienne* (Paris)
BZ	*Biblische Zeitschrift* (Paderborn)
CBQ	*Catholic Biblical Quarterly* (Washington DC)
Chr	*Christus* (Paris)

ChrM	*Christian Ministry* (Chicago IL)
ChS	*Church and Society* (New York)
CJT	*Canadian Journal of Theology* (Toronto)
Conci	*Concilium* (London)
CQ	*Covenant Quarterly* (Chicago)
Crux	*Crux* (Vancouver)
CT	*Christianity Today* (Washington DC)
CThM	*Currents in Theology and Mission* (St. Louis MO)
CTJ	*Calvin Theological Journal* (Grand Rapids MI)
CTQ	*Concordia Theological Quarterly* (Fort Wayne IN)
CTR	*Criswell Theological Review* (Dallas)
CuBi	*Cultura Bíblica* (Madrid)
CVia	*Communio Viatorum* (Prague)
Div	*Divinitas* (Rome)
DTT	*Dansk Teologisk Tidsskrift* (Cophenhagen)
EAJT	*East Asia Journal of Theology* (Singapore)
EB	*Estudios Bíblicos* (Madrid)
EE	*Estudios Eclesiásticos* (Madrid)
EGLMBS	*Eastern Great Lakes and Midwest Biblical Society* (Chicago)
EgT	*Église et théologie* (Ottawa)
EQ	*Evangelical Quarterly* (London)
EstT	*Estudios Teológicos* (Guatemala City)
ET	*Expository Times* (Edinburgh)
ETL	*Ephemerides Theologicae Lovanienses* (Louvain)
ETR	*Etudes Théologiques et Religieuses* (Montpellier)
EV	*Esprit et Vie* (Langres)
Evangel	*Evangel: A Quarterly Review of Biblical, Practical and Contemporary Theology* (Edinburgh)
EvJ	*Evangelical Journal* (Myerstown NJ)

EvT	*Evangelische Theologie* (Munich)
FilN	*Filologia Neotestamentaria* (Cordoba)
Found	*Foundations* (Rochester NY)
FundJ	*Fundamentalist Journal* (Lynchburg VA)
FV	*Foi et Vie* (Paris)
GeistL	*Geist und Leben* (Würzburg)
Greg	*Gregorianum* (Rome)
GTJ	*Grace Theological Journal* (Winona Lake IN)
HBT	*Horizons in Biblical Theology* (Pittsburg PA)
HTR	*Harvard Theological Review* (Cambridge MA)
HTS	*Hervormde Teologiese Studies* (Pretoria)
Impact	*Impact: A Journal of Thought of the Disciples of Christ on the Pacific Slope* (Singapore)
Int	*Interpretation* (Richmond VA)
IRM	*International Review of Mission* (London)
JBL	*Journal of Biblical Literature* (Atlanta)
JETS	*Journal of the Evangelical Theological Society* (Wheaton IL)
JMosP `	*Journal of the Moscow Patriarchate* (Moscow)
JRR	*Journal from the Radical Reformation* (Morrow GA)
JRT	*Journal of Religious Thought* (Washington DC)
JSNT	*Journal for the Study of the New Testament* (Sheffield)
JTS	*Journal of Theological Studies* (Oxford)
JTSA	*Journal of Theology for Southern Africa* (Rondebosch)
K	*Kairos: Zeitschrift für Religionswissenschaft und Theologie* (Salzburg)
LQ	*Lutheran Quarterly* (Gettysburg PA)
May	*Mayéutica* (Marcilla)
MS	*Mission Studies* (Leiden)
MSJ	*The Master's Seminary Journal* (Sun Valley CA)

NovT	*Novum Testamentum* (Leiden)
NRT	*La Nouvelle revue théologique* (Louvain)
NTS	*New Testament Studies* (Cambridge)
NTT	*Norsk teologisk tidsskrift* (Oslo)
NZSTR	*Neue Zeitschrift für systematisch Theologie und Religionsphilosophie* (Berlin)
OC	*One in Christ* (Turvey, Bedfordshire)
PEcc	*Pro Ecclesia* (Northfield MN)
Point	*Point* (Papua, New Guinea)
Pres	*Presbyterion* (St. Louis)
PRS	*Perspectives in Religious Studies* (Macon GA)
PSB	*Princeton Seminary Bulletin* (Princeton NJ)
RB	*Revue biblique* (Paris)
RBib	*Rivista Biblica* (Bologna)
RechSR	*Recherches de science religieuse* (Paris)
RevB	*Revista Biblica* (Buenos Aires)
RevExp	*Review and Expositor* (Louisville KY)
RHPR	*Revue d'histoire et de philosophie religieuses* (Strasbourg)
RivBib	*Rivista Biblica* (Brescia)
RJ	*Reformed Journal* (Grand Rapids MI)
RSB	*Religious Studies Bulletin* (Calgary)
RSPT	*Revue des Sciences Philosophiques et Théologiques* (Paris)
RTR	*Reformed Theological Review* (Melbourne)
Sale	*Salesianum* (Rome)
Salm	*Salmanticensis* (Salamanca)
SBLSP	*Society of Biblical Literature Seminar Papers* (Atlanta)
ScC	*Scuola cattolica: Rivista di scienze religiose* (Milan)
ScE	*Science et Esprit* (Montreal)
ScrB	*Scripture Bulletin* (Strawberry Hill, UK)

ScripT	*Scripta theologia* (Pamplona, Spain)
SE	*Sciences Ecclésiastiques* (Montreal)
SEAJT	*South East Asia Journal of Theology* (Singapore)
Semeia	*Semeia* (Atlanta)
SJT	*Scottish Journal of Theology* (Edinburgh)
SM	*Studia Missionalia* (Wuppertal-Barmen)
SMR	*Saint Mark's Review* (Canberra)
SR	*Studies in Religion/Sciences religieuses* (Waterloo)
StTheol	*Studia Theologica* (Copenhagen)
StudE	*Studia evangelica* (Berlin)
TD	*Theology Digest* (St. Louis)
Theology	*Theology* (London)
TLZ	*Theologische Literaturzeitung* (Leipzig)
TQ	*Theologische Quartalschift* (Tübingen)
TriJ	*Trinity Journal* (Deerfield IL)
TS	*Theological Studies* (Woodstock)
TT	*Theology Today* (Princeton NJ)
TTZ	*Trierer Theologische Zeitschrift* (Trier)
TynB	*Tyndale Bulletin* (Cambridge)
VC	*Vigiliae Christianae* (Leiden)
VD	*Verbum Domine* (Rome)
VerbC	*Verbum Caro: Revue théologique et oecuménique* (Neuchâtel)
VS	*La vie spirituelle* (Paris)
Way	*Way* (London)
WTJ	*Westminster Theology Journal* (Philadelphia)
WW	*Word and World* (St. Paul MN)
ZMiss	*Zeitschrift für Mission* (Basel)
ZNW	*Zeitschrift für die neutestamentliche Wissenschaft*
ZTK	*Zeitschrift für Theologie und Kirche*

PART ONE

Citations by Chapter and Verse

1:1-2:4

0001 G. Johnston, "The Life of the Christian in the World: An Exposition of Philippine 1:1-2:4," *CJT* 3 (1957): 248-54.

1:1-11

0002 Wendell R. Debner, "Christ and the Church: The Ministry of the Baptized," *WW* 7 (1987): 417-23.

1:1

0003 E. Best, "Bishops and Deacons: Philippians 1, 1," in *StudE* 4 (1968): 371-76.

0004 George W. Knight, "Two Offices and Two Orders of Elders: A New Testament Study," *Pres* 11 (1985): 1-12.

0005 David W. Miller, "The Uniqueness of New Testament Church Eldership," *GTJ* 6 (1985): 315-27.

0006 Theodore C. Skeat, "Did Paul Write to 'Bishops and Deacons' at Philippi? A Note on Philippians 1:1," *NovT* 37 (1995): 12-15.

1:3

0007 Leopold Sabourin, "Koinonia in the New Testament," *RSB* 1 (1981): 109-15.

0008 Ramón Trevijano Etchverria, "La mision en Tesalonica," *Salm* 32 (1985): 263-91.

1:4-11

0009 G. Gaide, "L'amour de Dieu en nous," *AsSeign* N.S. 6 (1969): 62-69.

1:4-6

0010 J. Mas, "Filipenses 1:4-6,8-11," *CuBi* 27 (1970): 343-46.

1:4

0011 G. P. Wiles, "The Divided Prayer-Report in Philippians," in *Paul's Intercessory Prayers: The Significance of the Intercessory Prayer Passages in the Letters of St. Paul.* Cambridge: University Press, 1974. Pp. 194-202.

1:5

0012 L.-M. Dewailly, " La part prise à l'Évangile (Phil. 1, 5)," *RB* 80 (1973): 247-60.

0013   Leopold Sabourin, "Koinonia in the New Testament," *RSB* 1 (1981): 109-15.

1:6-11

0014   F. Ogara, "Socios gaudii mei omnes vos esse," *VD* 15 (1935): 324-30.

0015   A. Sisti, "Nell'attesa del giorno di Cristo," *BibO* 7 (1965): 265-78.

1:6

0016   Alvin L. Baker, "Eternal Security Rightly Understood," *FundJ* 3 (1984): 18-20.

0017   Judith M. Gundry, *Paul and Perservence.* Luoisville: Westminster/John Knox, 1990.

0018   J. Gerald Janzen, "Creation and New Creation in Philippians 1:6," *HBT* 18 (1996): 27-54.

1:7

0019   Jacques Schlosser, "La communauté en charge de l'Evangile: A propos de Ph 1,7," *RHPR* 75 (1995): 67-76.

1:8-11

0020   J. Mas, "Filipenses 1:4-6,8-11," *CuBi* 27 (1970): 343-46.

1:8

0021   U. Holzmeister, "Viscera Christi," *VD* 16 (1936): 161-65.

0022   Ronald C. Sauer, "Should the Whole Bible Be Interpreted Literally," *FundJ* 3 (1984): 32-33.

1:9-11

0023   G. P. Wiles, "The Divided Prayer-Report in Philippians," in *Paul's Intercessory Prayers: The Significance of the Intercessory Prayer Passages in the Letters of St. Paul.* Cambridge: University Press, 1974. Pp. 194-202.

1:12-26

0024   Jean Perret, "Notes bibliques de prédication sur trois péricopes de l'Epître de saint Paul aux Philippiens," *VerbC* 19 (1965): 50-57.

1:12-13

0025   C. Ray Burchette, "Paul's Persecutions," *BI* 10/1 (1983): 66-71.

1:13

  0026   Siegbert Uhlig, "Textcritical Questions of the Ethiopic New Bible," in
          Alan S. Kaye, ed., *Semitic Studies* (festschrift for Wolf Leslau).
          Wiesbaden: Otto Harrassowitz, 1991. Pp. 1583-1600.

1:15-17

  0027   H. W. Bateman, "Were the Opponents at Philippi Necessarily Jewish,"
          BSac 155 (1998): 39-61.

1:15-16

  0028   J. H. Schütz, "The Normative Character of the Gospel: Philippians
          and 2 Corinthians," in *Paul and the Anatomy of Apostolic Authority*.
          SNTS #26. Cambridge: University Press, 1975. Pp. 159-86.

1:19-27

  0029   Wendell R. Debner, "Christ and the Church: The Ministry of the
          Baptized," *WW* 7 (1987): 417-23.

1:19-26

  0030   Thomas F. Dailey, "To Live or Die: Paul's Eschatological Dilemma
          in Philippians 1:19-26," *Int* 44 (1990): 18-28.

1:19-20

  0031   G. P. Wiles, "The Divided Prayer-Report in Philippians," in *Paul's
          Intercessory Prayers: The Significance of the Intercessory Prayer
          Passages in the Letters of St. Paul*. Cambridge: University Press,
          1974. Pp. 194-202.

1:20-27

  0032   C. Bigaré, "Soit que je vive, soit que je meure (Ph 1)," *AsSeign* N.S.
          56 (1974): 9-14.

1:20-24

  0033   G. Gappert, " 'Aufbrechen' und 'Bleiben'. Eine osterliche Besinnung
          zu Phil 1,20-24," *BL* 8 (1967): 63-67.

1:20

  0034   G. Bertram, " ἀποκαραδοκία," *ZNW* 49 (1958): 264-70.

  0035   D. R. Denton, "ἀποκαραδοκία," *ZNW* 73 (1982): 138-40.

1:21-26

0036   P. Hoffmann, "Das Mit-Christus-Sein im Tode nach Phil 1, 21-26," in
        *Die Toten in Christus: Eine religionsgeschichtliche und exegetische
        Untersuchung zur paulinischen Eschatologie*. München: Aschendorff,
        1972. Pp. 286-320.

0037   Arthur J. Droge, "Mori lucrum: Paul and Ancient Theories of
        Suicide," *NovT* 30 (1988): 263-86.

0038   Samuel Vollenweider, "Die Waagschalen von Leben und Tod: Zum
        antiken Hintergrund von Phil 1,21-26," *ZNW* 85 (1994): 93-115.

0039   James L. Jaquette, "Life and Death, Adiaphora, and Paul's Rhetorical
        Strategies," *NovT* 38 (1996): 30-54.

1:21-24

0040   André Feuillet, "Mort du Christ et mort du chrétien d'après les épitres
        pauliniennes," *RB* 66 (1959): 481-513.

1:21

0041   P. Joüon, "Notes philologiques sur quelques versets de l'épître aux
        Philippiens," *RechSR* 28 (1948): 88-93, 299-310.

0042   F. Wulf, "Denn Leben ist für mich Christus und Sterben ist Gewinn,"
        GeistL 30 (1957): 241-45.

0043   A. Giglioli, "Mihi enirn vivere Christus est," *RivBib* 16 (1968):
        305-16.

0044   D. W. Palmer, "To Die Is Gain (Philippians 1:21)," *NovT* 17 (1975):
        203-18.

0045   Anthony Bloom, "What It Means to Be a Christian according to St.
        Paul," *JMosP* 6 (1983): 73-75.

0046   Will K. Morris, "Rejoice Always," *ChrM* 16 (1985): 24.

1:22-23

0047   G. M. Lee, "Philippians 1:22-3," *NovT* 12 (1970): 361.

1:22

0048   Rodney R. Reeves, "To Be or Not to Be? That Is not the Question:
        Paul's Choice in Philippians 1:22," *PRS* 19 (1992): 273-89.

1:23-24
    0049 C.-J. De Vogel, "Reflexions on Philippians 1:23-24," *NovT* 19 (1977): 262-74.

1:23
    0050 X. Léon-Dufour, "Le visage aimé de la mort," in *Face à la mort: Jésus et Paul*. Paris: Seuil, 1979. Pp. 259-61.

    0051 Anne Hetzel, "L'accompagnement des mourants," *FV* 84 (1985): 29-45.

    0052 Anthony Hoekema, "Heaven: Not Just an Eternal Day off," *CT* 29 (1985): 18-19.

    0053 Günter Klein, "Aspekte ewigen Lebens im Neuen Testament: ein theologischer Annähungsversuch," *ZTK* 82 (1985): 48-70.

    0054 Will K. Morris, "Rejoice Always," *ChrM* 16 (1985): 24.

    0055 Enrique Treiyer, "S'en aller et etre avec Christ: Philippiens 1:23," *AUSS* 34 (1996): 47-64.

1:25
    0056 F.-J. Steinmetz and F. Wulf, "Ausharren und bleiben! Auslegung und Meditation von Lk 24,29; Jo 15,4 und Phil 1,25," *GeistL* 24 (1969): 225-29.

1:27-4:3
    0057 David E. Garland, "The Composition and Unity of Philippians: Some Neglected Literary Factors," *NovT* 27 (1985): 141-73.

1:27-2:18
    0058 James P. Berkeley, "Self-Emptying of the Church," *Found* 9 (1966): 70-74.

1:27-2:18
    0059 C. H. Giblin, "Exhortations to Christian Triumph Through Selfless Service," in *In Hope of God's Glory*. New York: Herder and Herder, 1970. Pp. 100-12.

1:27-30

>0060   V. C. Pfitzner, "Contending for the Faith - The Pale Athletic Termini,"
>in *Paul and the Agon Motif: Traditional Athletic Imagery in the
>Pauline Literature*. Leiden: Brill, 1967. Pp. 109-29.

>0061   Nikolaus Walter, "Christusgiaube und Heidnische Religiosität in
>Paulinischen Gemeinden," *NTS* 25 (1979): 422-42.

>0062   Edgar M. Krentz, "Military Language and Metaphors in Philippians,"
>in Bradley H. McLean, ed., *Origins and Method: Towards a New
>Understanding of Judaism and Christianity* (festschrift for John C.
>Hurd). Sheffield UK: JSOT Press, 1993. Pp. 105-27.

1:27-28

>0063   H. W. Bateman, "Were the Opponents at Philippi Necessarily Jewish,"
>*BSac* 155 (1998): 39-61.

>0064   G. W. Murray, "Paul's Corporate Witness in Philippians," *BSac* 155
>(1998): 316-26.

1:27

>0065   R. Roberts, "Old Texts in Modern Translations: Philippians 1:27," *ET*
>49 (1937-1938): 325-28.

>0066   R. R. Brewer, "The Meaning of *politeuesthe* in Philippians 1:27," *JBL*
>73 (1954): 76-83.

>0067   D. R. Hall, "Fellow-Workers with the Gospel," *ET* 85 (1973-1974):
>119-20.

>0068   E. C. Miller, "Politeuesthe in Philippians 1:27: Some Philological and
>Thematic Observations," *JSNT* 15 (1982): 86-96.

>0069   Sven Soderlund, "Focus on Philippians: A Review Article," *Crux* 20
>(1984): 27-32.

1:28

>0070   Gerald F. Hawthorne, "The Interpretation and Translation of
>Philippians 1:28b," *ET* 95 (1983): 80-81.

2:1-13

>0071   Ulrich Wilckens, "Das 'Carmen Christi' als Lied der Kirche:
>Meditation über Phil 2:1-13," in Angela Berlis and Klaus-Dieter

Gerth, eds., *Christus spes: Liturgie und Glaube im ökumenischer Kontext* (festschrift for Bischof Sigisbert Kraft). Frankfurt: Peter Lang, 1994. Pp. 321-34.

2:1-11

0072   Willaim Barclay "Philippians 2:1-11," *ET* 70 (1959-1960): 4-7, 40-44.

0073   Bo Reicke, "Unité chrétienne et diaconie, Phil. ii 1-11," in *Neotestamentica et Patristica* (festschrift for Oscar Cullmann). Leiden: Brill, 1962. Pp. 203-212.

0074   Jean Perret, "Notes bibliques de prédication sur trois péricopes de l'Epître de saint Paul aux Philippiens," *VerbC* 19 (1965): 50-57.

0075   James A. Sanders, "Dissenting Deities and Philippians 2:1-11," *JBL* 88 (1969): 279-90.

0076   Joachim Gnilka, "La carrière du Christ, appel à l'union et à la charité (Ph 2)," *AsSeign* N.S. 57 (1971): 12-19.

2:1-6

0077   Wendell R. Debner, "Christ and the Church: The Ministry of the Baptized," *WW* 7 (1987): 417-23.

0078   Douglas A. Templeton, "The Pauline Epistles as Border Ballads: Truth and Fiction in the Carmen Christi," in A. Graeme Auld, ed., *Understanding Poets and Prophets* (festschrift for George W. Anderson. Sheffield UK: JSOT Press, 1993. Pp. 350-65.

2:1-5

0079   Abdón Moreno García , "Aproximación al sentido de Filipenses 2,1-5," *EB* 47 (1989): 529-58.

2:1-4

0080   David A. Black, "Paul and Christian Unity: A Formal Analysis of Philippians 2:1-4," *JETS* 28 (1985): 299-308.

2:1

0081   Leopold Sabourin, "Koinonia in the New Testament," *RSB* 1 (1981): 109-15.

0082 Angelino S. Di Marco, "Koinonia pneumatos (2 Cor 13:13; Flp 2:1)--pneuma koinonias: circolaità e ambivalenza linguistica e filologica," *FilN* 1 (1988): 63-76.

2:2

0083 J. Randall O'Brien, "Like-Mindedness," *BI* 14/1 (1987): 27.

2:3

0084 Anthony Hoekema, "How We See Ourselves," *CT* 29 (1985): 36-38.

2:3-4

0085 Paul R. Fink, "Advice from the Apostle Paul," *FundJ* 4 (1985): 36.

2:5-11

0086 Ernst Käsemann, "Kritische Analyse von Phil. 2, 5-11," *ZTK* 47 (1950): 313-60.

0087 Charles M. Horne, "Let This Mind Be in You," *JETS* 3 (1960): 37-44.

0088 Christoph Barth, "True Servant: Philippians 2:5-11," *SEAJT* 6 (1965): 12-14.

0089 A. Sisti, "Sull'esempio di Cristo," *BibO* 7 (1965): 61-68.

0090 I. Howard Marshall, "The Christ-Hymn in Philippians," *TynB* 19 (1968): 104-27.

0091 John G. Gibbs, "Relation between Creation and Redemption according to Philippians 2:5-11," *NovT* 12 (1970): 270-83.

0092 C. F. D. Moule, "Further Reflexions on Philippians 2:5-11," in W. W. Gasque and R. P. Martin, eds., *Apostolic History and the Gospel* (festschrift for F. F. Bruce). Grand Rapids: Eerdmans, 1970. Pp. 264-76.

0093 Ulrich Browarzik, "Die dogmatische Frage nach der Göttlichkeit Jesu," *NZSTR* 13 (1971): 164-75.

0094 M. Hengel, *Der Sohn Gottes. Die Entstehung der Christologie und die jüdisch-hellenistische Religionsgeschichte.* Tübingen: Mohr, 1975.

0095 A. Ammassari, ""L'esaltazione del Cristo dopo la sua morte," in *La Resurrezione nella profeia, nelle apparizioni di Gesù*. 2 vols. Rome: Città Nuova Editrice, 1976. 2:54-58.

0096 K.-A. Bauer, "Der Weg der Diakonie. Predigt über Phil 2,5-1 1," *EvT* 36 (1976): 280-84.

0097 John G. Strelan, "Who Heals the Healers," *Point* 10 (1981): 170-79.

0098 Henk B. Kossen, "Der Friedensbegriff in der Bibel," in *Christen im Streit um den Frieden: Beiträge zu einer neuen Friedensethik*. Freiburg: Dreisam-Verlag, 1982. Pp. 36-47.

0099 Larry W. Hurtado, "Jesus as Lordly Example in Philippians 2:5-11," in Peter Richardson and John C. Hurd, eds., *From Jesus to Paul* (festschrift for Francis W. Beare). Waterloo: Wilfrid Laurier University Press, 1984. Pp. 113-26.

0100 David A. Black, "Paul and Christian Unity: A Formal Analysis of Philippians 2:1-4," *JETS* 28 (1985): 299-308.

0101 Albert Verwilghen, "Ph 2:5-11 dans l'oeuvre de Cyprien et dans les écrits d'auteurs anonymes africains du IIIIeme siécle," *Sale* 47 (1985): 707-34.

0102 L. D. Hurst, "Re-Enter the Pre-Existent Christ in Philippians 2:5-11," *NTS* 32 (1986): 449-57.

0103 Alphonse Maillot, "Les théologies de la mort du Christ chez Paul," *FV* 85 (1986): 33-45.

0104 Stephen W. Sykes, "The Strange Persistence of Kenotic Christology," in Alistair Kee and Eugene T. Long, eds., *Being and Truth* (festschrift for John Macquarrie). London: SCM Press, 1986. Pp. 349-75.

0105 John B. Webster, "Christology, Imitability and Ethics," *SJT* 39 (1986): 309-26.

0106 John B. Webster, "The Imitation of Christ," *TynB* 37 (1986): 95-120.

0107 N. T. Wright, "ἁρπαγμός and the Meaning of Philippians 2:5-11," *JTS* 37 (1986): 321-52.

0108   John Breck, "Biblical chiasmus: Exploring Structure for Meaning,"
       BTB 17 (1987): 70-74.

0109   François Rousseau, "Une disposition des versets de Philippiens
       2:5-11," *SR* 17 (1988): 191-98.

0110   Olaf Schumann, "Mission in der Weise Jesu Christi: Reflexionen im
       Anschluss an Phil 2:5-11," *ZMiss* 14 (1988): 168-71.

0111   Paul Trudinger, "Making Sense of the Ascension: The Cross as
       Glorification," *SMR* 133 (1988): 11-13.

0112   Alan Neely, "Mission as kenosis: Implications for Our Times," *PSB*
       N.S. 10 (1989): 202-23.

0113   Andrew Chester, "Jewish Messianic Expectations and Mediatorial
       Figures and Pauline Christology," in Martin Hengel and Ulrich
       Heckel, eds., *Paulus und das antike Judentum* (festschrift for Adolf
       Schlatter). Tübingen: Mohr, 1991. Pp. 17-89.

0114   James W. McClendon, "Philippians 2:5-11," *RevExp* 88 (1991):
       439-44.

0115   George W. E. Nickelsburg, "The Incarnation: Paul's Solution to the
       Universal Human Predicament," in Birger Pearson, et al., eds., *The
       Future of Early Christianity* (festschrift for Helmut Koester).
       Minneapolis: Fortress Press, 1991. Pp. 348-57.

0116   Hendrikus Boers and Donna Singles, trans. Louis Panier, "L'histoire
       de Jésus et le mythe du Christ," in Louis Panier, ed., *Le temps de la
       lecture: exégèse biblique et sémiotique* (festschrift for Jean Delorme).
       Paris, Cerf, 1993. Pp. 185-202

0117   Gerald Bostock, "Origen's Exegesis of the Kenosis Hymn," in Gilles
       Dorival and Alain Le Boulluec, eds., *Origeniana sexta: Origène et la
       Bible*. Louvain: Peeters, 1995. Pp. 531-47.

0118   Kenneth E. Bailey, " 'Inverted Parallelisms' and 'Encased Parables'
       in Isaiah and Their Significance for Old and New Testament
       Translation and Interpretation," in L. J. de Regt, et al., eds., *Literary
       Structure and Rhetorical Strategies in the Hebrew Bible*. Winona
       Lake IN: Eisenbrauns, 1996. Pp. 14-30.

0119   Robert J. Karris, *A Symphony of New Testament Hymns: Commentary on Philippians 2:5-11, Colossians 1:15-20, Ephesians 2:14-16, 1 Timothy 3:16, Titus 3:4-7, 1 Peter 3:18-22, and 2 Timothy 2:11-13*. Collegeville Mn: Liturgical Press, 1996.

0120   Veronica Koperski, *The Knowledge of Christ Jesus My Lord: The High Christology of Philippians 3:7-11*. Kampen: Kok Pharos, 1996.

0121   Robert A. Wortham, "Christology as Community: Identity in the Philippians Hymn--The Philippians Hymn as Social Drama," *PRS* 23 (1996): 269-87.

0122   Markus Bockmuehl, " 'The Form of God': Variations on a Theme of Jewish Mysticism," *JTS* N.S. 48 (1997): 1-23.

0123   Walter Brueggemann, "Neighborliness and the Limits of Power in God's Realm: On the Second 'Great Commandment'," *ChS* 87 (1997): 81-96.

0124   S. Wood, "Is Philippians 2:5-11 Incompatible with Feminist Concerns?" *PEcc* 6 (1997): 172-83.

0125   Ralph P. Martin and Brian J. Dodd, eds., *Where Christology Began: Essays on Philippians 2*. Louisville: Westminster/John Knox Press, 1998.

2:5-8

0126   J. Guillet "Forme du Christ et formation du chrétien, Philippiens," *Chr* 30 (1983): 82-87.

0127   Harold L. Wilmington, "Jesus Christ: The Misunderstood," *FundJ* 2 (1983): 42.

0128   Paul D. Hanson, "The Identity and Purpose of the Church," *TT* 42 (1985): 342-52.

0129   A. J. McClain, "The Doctrine of the Kenosis in Philippians 2:5-8," *MSJ* 9 (1998): 85-96.

2:5

0130   U. Holzmeister, "Hoc sentite in vobis, quod et in Christo Jesu," *VD* 22 (1942): 225-28.

0131 P. Joüon, "Notes philologiques sur quelques versets de l'épître aux
      Philippiens," *RechSR* 28 (1948): 88-93, 299-310.

0132 P. A. van Stempvoort, "De betekenis van Filippenzen 2:5 t/m 11,"
      NTT 19 (1964): 97-111.

0133 Andrew John Bandsta, "Adam and the Servant in Philippians 2:5ff,"
      CTJ 1 (1966): 213-16.

0134 L. A. Losie, "A Note on the Interpretation of Philippians 2:5," *ET* 90
      (1978): 52-53.

0135 Jacobus T. Bakker, "De tweevoudige gerechtigheid: Luthers 'sermo
      de duplici Iustitia', 1518," in Jacobus T. Bakker and J. P.
      Boendermaker, eds., *Luther na 500 jaar: teksten, vertaald en
      besproken.* Kampen: Kok, 1983. Pp. 30-57.

0136 D. T. Knapp, "The Self-Humiliation of Jesus Christ and Christ-Like
      Living: A Study of Philippians 2:6-11," *EvJ* 15 (1997): 80-94.

2:6

0137 W. Foerster, "Ouk arpagmon êgêsato bei den griechischen
      Kirchenvätern," *ZNW* 29 (1930): 115-28.

0138 A. Ehrhardt, "Nochmals: Ein antikes Herrscherideal," *EvT* 8
      (1948-1949): 569-72.

0139 H. Kruse, "ἁρπαγμός," *VD* 27 (1949): 355-60.

0140 H. Kruse, "Iterum 'ἁρπαγμός'," *VD* 29 (1951): 206-14.

0141 T. Arvedson, "Phil. 2,6 und Mt. 10,39," *StTheol* 5 (1952): 49-51.

0142 M. Laconi, "Non rapinam arbitratus est...," *RivBib* 5 (1957): 126-40.

0143 Ralph P. Martin, "Morphē in Philippians 2:6," *ET* 70 (1959-1960):
      183-84.

0144 David H. Wallace, "Note on Morphe," *TZ* 22 (1966): 19-25.

0145 Roy W. Hoover, "ἁρπαγμός Enigma: A Philological Solution," *HTR*
      64 (1971): 95-119.

0146 J. Carmignac, "L'Importance de la place d'une négation," *NTS* 18 (1971-1972): 131-66.

0147 Ceslaus Spicq, "Note sur morphe dans les papyrus et quelques inscriptions," *RB* 80 (1973): 37-45.

0148 Michael R. Austin, "Salvation and the Divinity of Jesus," *ET* 96 (1985): 271-75.

0149 Rolf Gögler, "Inkarnationsglaube und Bibeltheologie bei Origenes," *TQ* 165 (1985): 82-94.

0150 Walter Radl, "Alle Mühe umsonst: Paulus und der Gottesknecht," in Albert Vanhoye, *L'Apôtre Paul: personnalité, style et conception du ministère*. Leuven: Uitgeverij Peeters, 1986. Pp. 144-49.

0151 John Cochrane O'Neill, "Hoover on ἁρπαγμός Reviewed, with a Modest Proposal concerning Philippians 2:6," *HTR* 81 (1988): 445-49.

0152 Markus Bockmuehl, " 'The Form of God': Variations on a Theme of Jewish Mysticism," *JTS* N.S. 48 (1997): 1-23.

2:6-11

0153 R. Deichgräber, "Philipper 2,6-11," in *Gotteshymnus und Christushhymnus in der frühen Christenheit*. Göttingen: Vandenhoeck & Ruprecht, 1967. Pp. 118-33.

0154 C.-H. Hunzinger, "Zur Struktur der Christ us-Hyninen in Phil 2 und 1 Petr 3," in E. Lose, et al., eds., *Der Ruf Jesu und die Antwort der Gemeinde*. (festschrift for Joachim Jeremias). Göttingen: Vandenhoeck & Ruprecht, 1970. 142-56.

0155 F. Ogara, "Hoc sentite in vobis, quod et in Christo Iesu," *VD* 15 (1935): 99-109.

0156 A. A. Stephenson, "Christ's Self-abasernent," *CBQ* 1 (1939): 296-313.

0157 André Feuillet, "L'Homme-Dieu considéré dans sa condition terrestre," *RB* 51 (1942): 58-79.

0158   A. Ehrhardt "Jesus Christ and Alexander the Great," *JTS* 46 (1945): 45-51.

0159   V. Larrañaga, "El nombre sobre todo nombre dado a Jesús desde su Resurrección gloriosa," *EB* 6 (1947): 287-305.

0160   A. Ehrhardt, "Ein antikes Herrscherideal," *EvT* 8 (1948-1949): 101-10.

0161   J. Dupont, "Jésus-Christ dans son abaissement et son exaltation, d'après Phil., 2,6-11," *RechSR* 37 (1950): 500-14.

0162   L. Bouyer, " Arpagmos," in *Mélanges Jules Lebreton, RechSR* 39 (1951): 281-88.

0163   M. Meinertz, "Zum Verständnis des Christushymnus Phil. 2,5-11," *TTZ* 61 (1952): 186-92.

0164   A. Rolla, "Il passo Cristologico di Filipp. 2,5-11," *ScC* 80 (1952): 127-34.

0165   G. Perez, "Humillación y exaltación de Cristo," *CuBi* 13 (1956): 4-10, 84-88.

0166   J. M. Furness, "Arpagmos eauton ekenōse," *ET* 69 (1957-1958): 93-94.

0167   H. Lattanzi, "Cristo nella gerarchia degli esseri secondo le Lettere della cattività e quelle ai Romani," *Div* 2 (1958): 472-85.

0168   G. Bornkamm, "Zum Verständnis des Christus-Hymnus Phil 2,611," in *Studien zu Antike und Urchristentum: Gesammelte Aufsätze*. Múnich: Kaiser. 1959. Pp. 177-87.

0169   P. Dacquino, "Il testo cristologico di Fil. 2,6-11," *RivBib* 7 (1959): 221-29.

0170   L. Krinetzki, "Der Einfluss von Is 52,13-53,12 Par auf Phil 2,6-11," *TQ* 139 (1959): 157-93, 291-336.

0171   J. M. Furness, "The Authorship of Philippians ii. 6-11," *ET* 70 (1959-1960): 240-43.

0172 J. Jervell, "Zu Phil 2,6-11. Gott in Christus III. Die göttliche Würde Christi," in *Imago Dei*. FRLANT #76. Göttingen: Vandenhoeck & Ruprecht, 1960. Pp. 227-31.

0173 P. Neuenzeit, "Der Hymnus auf die Entäusserung Christi," *BK* 16 (1961): 9-13.

0174 D. M. Stanley, "A Palestinian Soteriological Theme: Christ as 'Ebed Yahweh. Phil. 2, 6 11)," in *Christ's Resurrection in Pauline Soteriology*. Rome: Pontifical Biblical Institute, 1961. Pp. 95-102.

0175 E. Larsson, *Christus als Vorbild: Eine Untersuchung zu den paulinischen Tauf- und Eikontexten.* Uppsala Almquist & Wiksells, 1962. Pp. 230-75.

0176 K. Wegenast, "Philippians 2:5-22," in *Das Verständnis der Tradition bei Paulus und in den Deuteropaulinen.* WMANT #8. Neukirchen-Vluyb: Neukirchener Verlag, 1962. Pp. 83-91.

0177 D. Georgi, "Der vorpaulinische Hymnus Phil 2, 6-11," in E. Dinkler, ed., *Zeit und Geschichte* (festschrift for Rudolf Bultmann). Tübingen: Mohr, 1964. Pp. 263-93.

0178 Ralph P. Martin, "The Form-Analysis of Philippians 2:5-11," *StudE* 2 (1964): 611-20.

0179 Georg Strecker, "Redaktion und Tradition im Christushymnus Phil 2:6-11," *ZNW* 55 (1964): 63-78.

0180 F. E. Vokes,"Arpagmos in Philippians 2:5-11," *StudE* 2 (1964): 670-75.

0181 André Feuillet, "L'hymne christologique de l'épître aux Philippiens 2:6-11," *RB* 72 (1965): 352-80, 481-507.

0182 André Feuillet, "L'hymne christologique de l'Epitre aux Philippiens 2:6-11," *RB* 72 (1965): 352-80.

0183 John Harvey, "New Look at the Christ Hymn in Philippians 2:6-11," *ET* 76 (1965): 337-39.

0184 L. Krinetzki, "Le serviteur de Dieu," *AsSeign* 37 (1965): 37-45.

0185 D. F. Hudson, "A Further Note on Philippians ii. 6-11," *ET* 77 (1965-1966): 29.

0186 Joseph Coppens, "Les affinités littéraires de l'hymne christologique Phil 2, 6-11," *ETL* 42 (1966): 238-41.

0187 M. Dhainaut, "Les abaissements volontaires du Christ: Philippiens 2,6-11," *BVC* 71 (1966): 44-57.

0188 E. B. F. Kinniburgh, "The Humily of God: A Discussion of Philippians 2: 6-11," *BT* 16 (1966): 16-19.

0189 Joseph Coppens, "Une nouvelle structuration de l'hymne christologique de l'Epître aux Philippiens," *ETL* 43 (1967): 197-202.

0190 Ralph P. Martin, *Carmen Christi: Philippians 2:5-11 in Recent Interpretation and in the Setting of Early Christian Worship.* SNTS #4. Cambridge: University Press, 1967.

0191 Charles H. Talbert, "Problem of Pre-existence in Philippians 2:6-11," *JBL* 86 (1967): 141-53.

0192 J. M. Furness, "Behind the Philippian Hymn," *ET* 79 (1967-1968): 178-82.

0193 Paul Trudinger, "Arpagmos and the Christological Significance of the Ascension," *ET* 79 (1967-1968): 279.

0194 Norman K. Bakken, "New Humanity: Christ and the Modern Age," *Int* 22 (1968): 71-82.

0195 D. W. B. Robinson, "Arnagmos: The Deliverance Jesus Refused?" *ET* 80 (1968-1969): 253-54.

0196 R. Schnackenburg, "Der Christushymnus Phil 2,6-11," in J, Feiner and M. Löhrer, eds., *Mysterium Salutis.* Volume 3. *Das Christusereignis.* Einsiedeln: Benziger, 1969. Pp. 309-22.

0197 André Feuillet, "L'épître aux Philippiens: hymne christologique," *AmCl* 80 (1970): 733-41.

0198 K. Gamber, "Der Christus-Hymnus im Philipperbrief in liturgiegeschichtlicher Sicht," *Bib* 51 (1970): 369-76.

0199 John G. Gibbs, "Philippians 2:6-11," in *Creation and Redemption: A Study in Pauline Theology*. Leiden: Brill, 1971. Pp. 73-92.

0200 Pierre Grelot, "Heurs et malheurs de la traduction liturgique," *EgT* 3 (1971): 449-59.

0201 J. T. Sanders, "Philippians ii. 6-11," in *The New Testament Christological Hymns: Their Historical and Religious Background*. SNTS #15. Cambridge: University Press, 1971. Pp. 9-12, 58-74.

0202 S. De Ausejo, "Es un himno a Cristo el prólogo de San Juan? Los himnos cristologicos de la Iglesia primitiva y el prólogo del IV Evangelio," in *La escatologia individual neotestamentana a la luz de las ideas en los tiempos apostolicos*. Madrid: Consejo Superior de Investigaciones Científicas, 1972. Pp. 307-96.

0203 Pierre Grelot, "Deux notes critiques sur Philippiens 2,6-11," *Bib* 54 (1973): 169-96.

0204 B. Rigaux, "Ph, 2.6-11," in *Dieu l'a ressuscité: Exégèse et théologie biblique*. Gembloux: Duculot, 1973. Pp. 147-54.

0205 Georg Strecker, "Freiheit und Agape. Exegese und Predigi 6her Phil 2,5-11," in H. D. Betz and L. Schottroff, eds., *Neues Testament und christliche Existenz* (festschrift for Herbert Braun). Tübingen: Mohr, 1973. Pp. 523-38.

0206 Thomas F. Glasson, "Two notes on the Philippians hymn 2:6-11," *NTS* 21 (1974): 133-39.

0207 Bruno Corsani, "Gesù Cristo è il Signore," in Maria Vingiani, et al., eds., *Ecumenismo oggi: bilancio e prospettive: atti della XIII Sessione di formaziona ecumenica*. Turin: Elle Di Ci, 1975. Pp. 195-205.

0208 P. Dacquino, "L'umiltà e l'esaltazione dell'Adamo escatologico," *BibO* 17 (1975): 241-51.

0209 M. D. Hooker, "Philippians 2:6-11," in Earle Ellis and Erich Grässer, eds., *Jesus und Paulus* (festschrift for Georg W. Kümmel). Göttingen: Vandenhoeck & Ruprecht, 1975. Pp. 151-64.

0210   J. Thomas, "L'Hymne de l'Épître aux Philippiens," *CHR* 22 (1975): 334-45.

0211   O. Hofius, *Der Christushymnus Philipper 2,6-11: Untersuchungen zu Gestalt und Aussage eines urchristlichen Psalms.* WUNT #17. Tübingen: Mohr, 1976.

0212   Jerome Murphy-O'Connor, "Christological Anthropology in Philippians 11:6-11," *RB* 83 (1976): 25-50.

0213   F. Manns, *Essais sur le Judéo-Christianisme.* SBFLA #12. Jerusalem: Franciscan Printing Press, 1977.

0214   George Howard, "Philippians 2:6-11 and the Human Christ," *CBQ* 40 (1978): 368-87.

0215   H.-M. Schenke, "Die Tendenz der Weisheit zur Gnosis," in Barbara Aland, ed., *Gnosis* (festschrift for Hans Jonas). Göttingen: Vandenhoeck & Ruprecht, 1978. Pp. 351-72.

0216   A. Viard, "Abaissement et élévation du Christ Jésus," *EV* 78 (1978): 57-59.

0217   Harald Hegermann, "Der erhöhte Herr in der exegetisch gesichteten neutestamentlichen Darstellung," in Heinrich Kahlefeld, ed., *Schriftauslegung dient dem Glauben.* Frankfurt: Knecht, 1979. Pp. 35-55.

0218   Bertold Klappert, "Arbeit Gottes und Mitarbeit des Menschen," in Jürgen Moltmann, ed., *Recht auf Arbeit, Sinn der Arbeit.* Münich: Kaiser Verlag, 1979. Pp. 84-134.

0219   E. Lupoeri, "La morte di Croce: Contributi per un'analisi di Fil. 2,6-11," *RBib* 27 (1979): 271-311.

0220   B. Eckman, "A Quantitative Metrical Analysis of the Philippians Hymn," *NTS* 26 (1980): 258-66.

0221   W. Grundmann, *Wandlungen im Verständnis des Heils. Drei nachgelassene Aufsätze zur Theologie des Neuen Testaments.* Arbeiten zur Theologie #65. Stuttgart: Calwer, 1980.

0222 Nicolas Ozoline, "Quelques images relatives à la célébration primitive de la cinquantaine pascale," in Achille M. Triacca and A. Pistoia, eds., *L'église dans la liturgie*. Rome: CLV - Edizioni Liturgiche, 1980. Pp. 231-53.

0223 C. J. Robbins, "Rhetorical Structure of Philippians 2:6-11," *CBQ* 42 (1980): 73-82.

0224 A. Spreafico, "Theos/anthrōpos: Fil. 2,6-11," *RBib* 28 (1980): 407-15.

0225 A. O'Leary, "The Mystery of Our Religion," *Way* 21 (1981): 243-54.

0226 H. W. Bartsch, "Der Christushymnus Phil. 2,6-11 und der historische Jesus," *StudE* 7 (1982): 21-30.

0227 J.-C. Basset, "Théologie de la croix et culture indienne. L'interprétation de V. Chakkarai à la lumière de Philippiens 2:6-11," *RHPR* 63 (1983): 417-34.

0228 Joachim Gnilka, "Der Christushymnus des Philipperbriefes (2,6-11) und die neutestamentliche Hymnendichtung," in Hans Becker and Reiner Kaczynski, eds., *Liturgie und Dichtung: Ein interdisziplinäres Kompendium, I: Historische Präsentation*. Sankt Ottilien: EOS Verlag, 1983. Pp. 173-85.

0229 T. Nagata, "A Neglected Literary Feature of the Christ-Hymn in Philippians 2:6-11," *AJBI* 9 (1983): 184-229.

0230 A. Viard, "Jésus crucifié, Seigneur du monde (Ph 2,6-11)," *EV* 83 (1983): 79-80.

0231 Norman K. Bakken, "Uma nova criaçao: o Cristo para o nosso tempo," *EstT* 24 (1984): 118-28.

0232 D. M. Stanley, "Imitation in Paul's Letters: Its Significance for His Relationship to Jesus and to His Own Christian Foundations," in Peter Richardson and John C. Hurd, eds., *From Jesus to Paul* (festschrift for Francis W. Beare). Waterloo: Wilfrid Laurier University Press, 1984. Pp. 127-41.

0233 Byung-Mu Ahn, "The Body of Jesus-Event Tradition," *EAJT* 3 (1985): 293-309.

0234   Antonio M. Artola, "La mística cristopática de San Pablo de la Cruz,"
       EE 60 (1985): 135-56.

0235   Jean Marc Laporte, "Kenosis and koinonia: The Path Ahead for
       Anglican-Roman Catholic Dialogue," *OC* 21 (1985): 102-20.

0236   Franz Mussner, "Das Reich Christi: Bemerkungen zur Eschatologie
       des Corpus Paulinum," in Michael Böhnke and Hanspeter Heinz, eds.,
       *Im Gespräch mit dem dreieinen Gott: Elemente einer trinitarischen
       Theologie* (festschrift for Wilhelm Breuning). Düsseldorf: Patmos
       Verlag, 1985. Pp. 141-55.

0237   Christophe Senft, "Paul et Jésus," *FV* 84 (1985): 49-56.

0238   Albert Verwillghen, "Le Christ Jésus, source de l'humilité chrétienn
       (Phil 2,6-8)," in Anne-Marie La Bonnardière, ed., *Saint Augustin et
       la Bible*. Paris: Editions Beauchesne, 1986. Pp. 427-37.

0239   Guy Wagner, "Le scandale de la croix expliqué par le Chant du
       Serviteur d'Esaïe 53." Réflexion sur Philippiens 2:6-11," *ETR* 61
       (1986): 177-87.

0240   Teresia Yai-Chow Wong, "The Problem of Pre-existence in
       Philippians 2:6-11," *ETL* 62 (1986): 267-82.

0241   Pheme Perkins, "Christology, Friendship and Status: The Rhetoric of
       Philippians," *SBLSP* 26 (1987): 509-20.

0242   Mathias Rissi, "Der Christushymnus in Phil 2,6-11," in Wolfgang
       Haase, ed., *Principat 25, 4: Religion*. New York: Walter de Gruyter,
       1987. Pp. 3315-26.

0243   Charles A. Wanamaker, "Philippians 2:6-11: Son of God or Adamic
       Christology?" *NTS* 33 (1987): 179-93.

0244   David A. Black, "The Authorship of Philippians 2:6-11: Some
       Literary-Critical Observations," *CTR* 2 (1988): 269-89.

0245   Joseph A. Fitzmyer, "The Aramaic Background of Philippians
       2:6-11," *CBQ* 50 (1988): 470-83.

0246   Ulrich B. Müller, "Der Christushymnus Phil 2:6-11," *ZNW* 79 (1988):
       17-44.

0247   Nikolaus Walter, "Geschichte und Mythos in der urchristlichen
        Präexistenzchristologie," in Hans H. Schmid, ed., *Mythos und
        Rationalität.* Gütersloh: Gütersloher Verlaghaus Mohn, 1988. Pp.
        224-34.

0248   Jan Botha, "Die Kolossense-himne (Kol 1:15-20)," *HTS* suppl 1
        (1989): 54-82.

0249   Sheila Briggs, "Can an Enslaved God Liberate? Hermeneutical
        Reflections on Philippians 2:6-11," *Semeia* 47 (1989): 137-53.

0250   Mark A. Filbert, "An Analysis of 'All Praise to Thee, for Thou, O
        King Divine' and 'At the Name of Jesus' in Relation to Philippians
        2:6-11," *Hymn* 40 (1989): 12-15.

0251   Michel Gourgues, "La foi chrétienne primitive face à la croix: le
        témoignage des formulaires pré-pauliniens," *ScE* 41 (1989): 49-69.

0252   A. H. Snyman, "Die Filippense-himne (Fil 2:6-11)," *HTS* suppl 1
        (1989): 44-53.

0253   Edgar Haulotte, "Formation du corpus du Nouveau Testament:
        recherche d'un 'module' génératif intratextuel," in Christoph
        Theobald, ed., *Le canon des Ecritures: études historiques,
        exégétiques et systématiques.* Paris: Editions du Cerf, 1990. Pp.
        255-439.

0254   Paul S. Minear, "Singing and Suffering in Philippi," in Robert T.
        Fortna and Beverly R. Gaventa, eds., *The Conversation Continues:
        Studies in Paul & John* (festschrift for Louis Martyn). Nashville:
        Abingdon Press, 1990. Pp. 202-19.

0255   L. Michael White, "Morality between Two Worlds: A Paradigm of
        Friendship in Philippians," in David L. Balch, et als., eds., *Greeks,
        Romans, and Christians* (festschrift for Abraham J. Malherbe).
        Minneapolis: Fortress Press, 1990. Pp. 201-15.

0256   Roselyne Dupont-Roc, "De l'hymne christologique à une vie de
        koinonia: Etude sur la lettre aux Philippiens," *EB* 49 (1991): 451-72.

0257   Wayne A. Meeks, "The Man from Heaven in Paul's Letter to the
        Philippians," in Birger Pearson, et al., eds., *The Future of Early*

Christianity (festschrift for Helmut Koester). Minneapolis: Fortress Press, 1991. Pp. 329-36.

0258   C. Basevi and Juan Chapa, "Philippians 2:6-11: The Rhetorical Function of a Pauline 'Hymn'," in Stanley E. Porter, and Thomas H. Ibricht, eds., *Rhetoric and the New Testament*. Sheffield UK: JSOT Press, 1993. Pp. 338-56.

0259   Steven J. Kraftchick, "A Necessary Detour: Paul's Metaphorical Understanding of the Philippian Hymn," *HBT* 15 (1993): 1-37.

0260   Roland Bergmeier, "Weihnachten mit und ohne Glanz: Notizen zu Johannesprolog und Philipperhymnus," *ZNW* 85 (1994): 47-68.

0261   Robert H. Gundry, "Style and Substance in 'the Myth of God Incarnate' according to Philippians 2:6-11," in Stanley E. Porter, et al., eds., *Crossing the Boundaries: Essays in Biblical Interpretation* (festschrift for Michael D. Goulder). Leiden: E. J. Brill, 1994. Pp. 271-93.

0262   H. Navarro Cuervo, "La kénosis de Cristo," *May* 22 (1996): 339-436.

0263   S. A. Deane, "Obedience and Humility of the Second Adam: Philippians 2:6-11," *JRR* 1 (1997): 4-12.

0264   D. T. Knapp, "The Self-Humiliation of Jesus Christ and Christ-Like Living: A Study of Philippians 2:6-11," *EvJ* 15 (1997): 80-94.

0265   C. Basevi, "Estudio literario y teológico del himno cristológico de la epístola a los Filipenses (Phil 2,6-11)," *ScripT* 30 (1998): 439-72.

2:6-9

0266   Paul Gilbert, "La christologie sotériologique de Kant," *Greg* 66 (1985): 491-515.

2:6-8

0267   Albert Verwilghen, "Ph 2:6-8 dans l'oeuvre de Tertullien," *Sale* 47 (1985): 433-65.

0268   Masahirô Tomura, "Yasukuni und Evangelium: Predigt nach Phil 2,6-8," in Yoshiki Terazono and Heyo E. Hamer, eds., *Brennpunkte in Kirche und Theologie Japans: Beiträge und Dokumente*. Neukirchen-Vluyn: Neukirchener Verlag, 1988. Pp. 99-106.

0269 D. T. Knapp, "The Self-Humiliation of Jesus Christ and Christ-Like Living: A Study of Philippians 2:6-11," *EvJ* 15 (1997): 80-94.

2:6-7

0270 D. R. Griffiths, "Arpagmos and eauton ekenōsen in Philippians 2:6-7," *ET* 69 (1957-1958): 237-39.

0271 W. Powell, "Arpagmos eauton ekenōsen," *ET* 71 (1959-1960): 88.

0272 Pierre Grelot, "La traduction et l'interprétation de Ph 2, 6-7. Quelques éléments d'enquête patristique," *NRT* 93 (1971): 897-922; 1009-26.

0273 Pierre Grelot, "Deux expressions difficiles de Philippiens 2:6-7," *Bib* 53 (1972): 495-507.

0274 Joe Gaquare, "Indigenisation as incarnation: the concept of a Melanesian Christ," *Point* 6 (1977): 146-53.

0275 Robert Gromacki, "The Virgin Birth," *FundJ* 1 (1982): 17-19.

0276 Hermann Binder, "Erwgungen zu Phil 2:6-7b," *ZNW* 78/3 (1987): 230-43.

0277 Florence M. Gillman, "Another Look at Romans 8:3: 'In the Likeness of Sinful Flesh'," *CBQ* 49 (1987): 597-604.

0278 Albert Verwilghen, "Le Christ médiateur selon Ph 2,6-7 dans l'oeuvre de saint Augustin," in Bernard Bruning, et al., eds., *Collectanea Augustiniana* (festshcrift for T. J. van Bavel). Volume 2. Louvain: Leuven University Press, 1990. Pp. 469-82.

0279 Alberto Viciano, "Aspects christologiques du 'Corpus Paulinum' dans la controverse antimanichéenne de Saint Augustin," in Alois van Tongerloo and Soren Giversen, eds., *Manichaica selecta* (festschrift for Julien Ries. Louvain: International Association of Manichaean Studies, 1991. Pp. 379-89.

2:7-9

0280 S. Zedda, "La povertà di Cristo secondo S. Paolo," in *Evangelizare pauperibus*. Brescia: Paideia, 1978. Pp. 343-69.

2:7-8

      0281   Frank Chikane, "The Incarnation in the Life of the People in Southern Africa," *JTSA* 51 (1985): 37-50.

2:7

      0282   Joachim Jeremias, "Zu Phil 2:7: Heauton ekenosen," *NovT* 6 (1963): 182-88.

      0283   Joseph Coppens, "Phil 2:7 et Is 53:12, le problème de la 'kénose'," *ETL* 41 (1965): 147-50.

      0284   P. Schoonenberg, "Il s'anéantit Lui-même," *Conci* 11 (1966): 45-60.

      0285   F. Wulf, "Gott im Menschen Jesus. Auslegung und Meditation von Jo 1,14; Phil 2,7; Lk 2,11," *GeistL* 42 (1969): 472-73.

      0286   U. Vanni, " 'Homoiōma' in Paolo: Un'interpretazione esegetico-teologica alla luce dell'uso dei LXX," *Greg* 58 (1977): 321-45; 431-70.

      0287   A. Vicent Cernuda, "La génesis humana de Jesucristo según S. Pablo," *EstB* 37 (1978): 57-77; 267-89.

      0288   Florence M. Gillman, "Another Look at Romans 8:3: 'In the Likeness of Sinful Flesh'," *CBQ* 49 (1987): 597-604.

2:8

      0289   G. Lefebvre, "La croix, mystère d'obéissance," *VS* 96 (1957): 339-48.

      0290   Marcel Doucet, "La volonté humaine du Christ, spécialement en son agonie: Maxime le Confesseur, interprète de l'Ecriture," *ScE* 37 (1985): 123-59.

2:9-11

      0291   Siefried Wagner, "Das Reich des Messias: zur Theologie der alttestamentlichen Königspsalmen," *TLZ* 109 (1984): 865-74.

      0292   L. J. Kreitzer and D. W. Rrook, " 'Singing in a New Key.' Philippians 2:9-11 and the 'Andante' of Beethoven's Kreutzer Sonata," *ET* 109 (1998): 231-33.

2:9-10

      0293   David L. Balas, "The Meaning of the 'Cross'," in Andreas Spira and Christoph Klock, eds., *The Easter Sermons of Gregory of Nyssa:*

Translation and Commentary. Cambridge: Philadelphia Patristic Foundation, 1981. Pp. 305-18.

2:9

0294 Ian G. Scott, "Jesus is Lord," *ET* 96 (1985): 305-307.

2:10-11

0295 Frank Stagg, "The Name 'Jesus'," *BI* 14/1 (1987): 73.

2:10

0296 Geevarghese Osthathios, "Conviction of Truth and Tolerance of Love," *IRM* 74 (1985): 490-96.

2:11-13

0297 J. C. Campbell, "The Christian and His Life-Style," *ET* 92 (1981): 314-15.

2:11

0298 W. Thüsing, "Die Inthronisation Christi als des Kyrios zur Verherrlichung Gottes," in *Per Chiistum in Deum: Studien zum Verhältnis von Christozentrik und Theozentrik in den paulinischen Hauptbriefen.* Münich: Aschendorf, 1965. Pp. 46-60.

0299 K. Gamber, "In gloria est Dei Patris. Zu einer Textänderung in der Neo-Vulgata," *BZ* 24 (1980): 262-66.

2:12-19

0300 Joseph R. Jeter "Sermons on the fruit of the Spirit," *Impact* 15 (1985): 1-64.

2:12-18

0301 E. Fuchs, "Andacht über Philipper 2:12-18," *EvT* 7 (1947-1948): 97-98.

0302 Ernst Käsemann, "Philipper 2, 12-18," in *Exegelische Versucbe und Besinnungen.* Göttingen: Vandenhoeck & Ruprecht, 1960. 1:293-298.

0303 Sven Soderlund, "Focus on Philippians: A Review Article," *Crux* 20 (1984): 27-32.

2:12-13

0304 P. Joüon, "Notes philologiques sur quelques versets de l'épître aux Philippiens," *RechSR* 28 (1948): 88-93, 299-310.

0305 R. C. Sproul, "Heresies of Holiness," *CT* 30 (1965): 30-31.

0306 S. Pedersen, "Mit Furcht und Zittern (Phil. 2,12-13)," *StTheol* 32 (1978): 1-31.

0307 Norbert Baumert, "Wirket euer Heil mit Furcht und Zittern (Phil 2,12f)," *GeistL* 52 (1979): 1-9.

0308 Anthony Hoekema, "Created Persons," *RJ* 36 (1986): 8-11.

0309 Beat Weber, "Philipper 2,12-13: Text - Kontext - Intertext," *BibN* 85 (1996): 31-37.

2:12

0310 Otto Glombitza, "Mit Furcht und Zittern - zum Verständnis von Philip. 2:12," *NovT* 3 (1959-1960): 100-106.

0311 Peter von der Osten-Sacken, "Heil für die Juden - auch ohne," in Hans-Georg Geyer, et al., eds., *"Wenn nicht jetzt, wann dann"* (festschrift for Hans-Joachim Kraus). Neukirchen-Vluyn: Neukirchener Verlag, 1983. Pp. 169-82.

0312 Michael Parsons, "Being Precedes Act: Indicative and Imperative in Paul's Writing," *EQ* 60 (1988): 99-127.

0313 Jost Eckert, "Mit Furcht und Zittern wirkt euer Heil: zur Furcht vor Gott als christlicher Grundhaltung," in Johannes J. Degenhardt, ed., *Die Freude an Gott - unsere Kraft* (festschrift for Otto B. Knoch). Stuttgart: Verlag Katholisches Bibelwerk, 1991. Pp. 262-70.

2:13

0314 W. H. Robinson, "Your Life has a Plan," *ET* 88 (1976): 79-80.

2:14-17

0315 Richard D. Patterson, "Laboring for Christ," *FundJ* 4 (1985): 67.

2:14-16

0316 G. W. Murray, "Paul's Corporate Witness in Philippians," *BSac* 155 (1998): 316-26.

2:15

0317 S. K. Finlayson, "Lights, Stars or Beacons," *ET* 77 (1966): 181.

2:16

0318 V. C. Pfitzner, "Lest I Run or Have Run in Vain," in *Paul and the Agon Motif: Traditional Athletic Imagery in the Pauline Literature*. Leiden: Brill, 1967. Pp. 99-108.

0319 J. Duncan M. Derrett, "Running in Paul: The Midrashic Potential of Hab 2:2," *Bib* 66 (1985): 560-67.

2:17-18

0320 Richard D. Patterson, "Pouring out," *FundJ* 2 (1983): 19.

0321 B. P. Robinson, "Paul's Character in the Face of Death," *ScrB* 28 (1998): 77-87.

2:17

0322 Claude Tassin, "L'apostolat, un 'Sacrifice'? Judaïsme et métaphore paulinienne," in Marcel Neusch, ed., *Le sacrifice dans les religions*. Pp. 85-116.

0323 U. Holzmeister, " 'Gaudete in Domino semper' et 'beati qui lugent'," *VD* 22 (1942): 257-62.

0324 A.-M. Denis, "Versé en libation. Versé en son sang?" *RechSR* 45 (1957): 567-70.

0325 A.-M. Denis, "La fonction apostolique et la liturgie nouvelle en esprit," *RSPT* 42 (1958): 617-50.

0326 R. Corriveau, *The Liturgy of Life: A Study of the Ethical Thought of St. Paul in His Letters to the Early Christian Communities*. Paris: Desclée de Brouwer, 1970. Pp. 111-17.

0327 Richard D. Patterson, "The Service of Faith," *FundJ* 4 (1985): 50.

0328 David G. Peterson, "Further Reflections on Worship in the New Testament," *RTR* 44 (1985): 34-41.

2:20

0329 P. Joüon, "Notes philologiques sur quelques versets de l'épître aux Philippiens," *RechSR* 28 (1948): 88-93, 299-310.

0330 Panayotis Christou, "ἰσόψυχος, Phil. 2:20," *JBL* 70 (1951): 293-96.

2:22

0331 G. W. Murray, "Paul's Corporate Witness in Philippians," *BSac* 155 (1998): 316-26.

2:25-30

0332 Bernhard Mayer, "Paulus als Vermittler zwischen Epaphroditus und der Gemeinde von Philippi: Bemerkungen zu Phil 2:25-30," *BZ* N.S. 31 (1987): 176-88.

0333 G. W. Murray, "Paul's Corporate Witness in Philippians," *BSac* 155 (1998): 316-26.

2:26-27

0334 Peter Jensen, "Faith and Healing in Christian Theology," *Point* 11 (1982): 153-59.

2:27

0335 Will K. Morris, "Rejoice Always," *ChrM* 16 (1985): 24.

2:30

0336 H. J. De Jonge, "Eine Konjektur Joseph Scaligers zu Philipper ii 30," *NovT* 17 (1975): 297-302.

0337 David G. Peterson, "Further Reflections on Worship in the New Testament," *RTR* 44 (1985): 34-41.

3:1-15

0338 Jean Perret, "Notes bibliques de prédication sur trois péricopes de l'Epître de saint Paul aux Philippiens," *VerbC* 19 (1965): 50-57.

3:1

0339 P. Joüon, "Notes philologiques sur quelques versets de l'épître aux Philippiens," *RechSR* 28 (1948): 88-93, 299-310.

0340 M. Zerwick, "Gaudium et pax custodia cordium," *VD* 31 (1953): 101-104.

3:2-4:13

0341 Aida B. Spencer, *Paul's* Literary Style: A Stylistic and Historical Comparison of 2 Corinthians 11:16-12:13, Romans 8:9-39, and Philippians 3:2-4:13. Lanham Md: University Press of America, 1998.

3:2-4:3
    0342   Detlev Dormeyer, "The Implicit and Explicit Readers and the Genre of Philippians 3:2-4:3, 8-9: Response to the Commentary of Wolfgang Schenk," *Semeia* 48 (1989): 147-59.

3:2-4:1
    0343   C. H. Giblin, "Apostolic Christian Perfection," in *In Hope of God's Glory.* New York: Herder and Herder, 1970. Pp. 113-17.

    0344   G. P. Wiles, "Apostolic Christian Perfection," in *Paul's Intercessory Prayers: The Significance of the Intercessory Prayer Passages in the Letters of St. Paul.* Cambridge: University Press, 1974. Pp. 101-107.

3:2-21
    0345   John Reumann, "Justification and the imitatio motif in Philippians," in George H. Anderson and James R. Crumley, eds., *Promoting Unity: Themes in Lutheran-Catholic Dialogue* (festschrift for Johannes Cardinal Willebrands). Minneapolis: Augsburg Fortress, 1989. Pp. 17-28.

    0346   David A. DeSilva, "No Confidence in the Flesh: The Meaning and Function of Philippians 3:2-21," *TriJ* 15 (1994): 27-54.

    0347   Darrell J. Doughty, "Citizens of Heaven: Philippians 3:2-21," *NTS* 41 (1995): 102-22.

3:2-17
    0348   Stephen E. Fowl, "Who's Characterizing Whom and the Difference This Makes: Locating and Centering Paul," *SBLSP* 32 (1993): 537-53.

3:2-16
    0349   D. M. Stanley, "Imitation in Paul's Letters: Its Significance for His Relationship to Jesus and to His Own Christian Foundations," in Peter Richardson and John C. Hurd, eds., *From Jesus to Paul* (festschrift for Francis W. Beare). Waterloo: Wilfrid Laurier University Press, 1984. Pp. 127-41.

3:2-14
    0350   Ulrich Schoenborn, "El yo y los demas en el discurso paulino," *RevB* 51 (1989): 163-80.

3:2-11

0351 R. C. Tannehill, "Philippians 3,2-11," in *Dying and Rising with Christ: A Study in Pauline Theology*. Berlin: Töpelmann, 1967. Pp. 114-23.

0352 Robert H. Gundry, "Grace, Works, and Staying Saved in Paul," *Bib* 66 (1985): 1-38.

0353 Marion L. Soards, "The Righteousness of God in the Writings of the Apostle Paul," *BTB* 15 (1985): 104-109.

0354 Heikki Räisänen, "Paul's Conversion and the Development of His View of the Law," *NTS* 33 (1987): 404-19.

3:2-7

0355 Benjamin Fiore, "Invective in Romans and Philippians," *EGLMBS* 10 (1990): 181-89.

3:2-6

0356 Pierre Bonnard, "Conversation biblique avec Jean Delumeau," *FV* 84 (1985): 77-81.

3:2

0357 G. D. Kilpatrick, "Blepete: Philippians 3,2," in M. Black and G. Fohrer, eds., *In Memoriam Paul Kahle* (festschrift for Paul Kahle). Berlin: Töpelmann, 1968. Pp. 146-48.

0358 Sven Soderlund, "Focus on Philippians: A Review Article," *Crux* 20 (1984): 27-32.

0359 Kenneth Grayston, "The Opponents in Philippians 3," *ET* 97 (1986): 170-72.

3:3-11

0360 Ulrich Luck, "Die Bekehrung des Paulus und das paulinische Evangelium: zur Frage der Evidenz in Botschaft und Theologie des Apostels," *ZNW* 76 (1985): 187-208.

3:3-5

0361 H. R. Moehring, "Some Remarks on sarks in Philippians 3:3," *StudE* 4 (1968): 432-36.

3:3

0362 Wolfgang Schrage, "Israel nach dem Fleisch," in Hans-Georg Geyer, et al., eds., *"Wenn nicht jetzt, wann dann"* (festschrift for Hans-Joachim Kraus). Neukirchen-Vluyn: Neukirchener Verlag, 1983. Pp. 143-51.

0363 A. Boyd Luter, "Worship as Service: The New Testament Usage of latreuo," *CTR* 2 (1988): 335-44.

3:4-11

0364 J. Guillet "Forme du Christ et formation du chrétien, Philippiens," *Chr* 30 (1983): 82-87.

0365 E. P. Sanders, "Paul on the Law, His Opponents, and the Jewish People in Philippians 3 and 2 Corinthians ii," in Peter Richardson David Granskou, eds., *Anti-Judaism in Early Christianity*. Volume 1: *Paul and the Gospels*. Waterloo: Wilfred Laurier Press, 1986. Pp. 75-90.

3:4

0366 G. Baumbach, "Antijudaismus im Neuen Testament: Fragestellung und Lösungsmöglichkeit," *K* 25 (1983): 68-85.

3:5-6

0367 William O. Walker, "Acts and the Pauline Corpus Reconsidered," *JSNT* 24 (1985): 3-23.

3:5

0368 John T. Greene, "Paul's Hermeneutic Versus Its Competitors," *JRT* 42 (1985): 7-21.

0369 P. Joüon, "Notes philologiques sur quelques versets de l'épître aux Philippiens," *RechSR* 28 (1948): 88-93, 299-310.

3:6-11

0370 J. Blank, "Phil 3,6-11," in *Paulus und Jesus: Eine theologische Grundlegung*. StABT #18. Münich: Kösel, 1968. Pp. 231-38.

3:6

0371 M. Goguel, "Kats dikaiosunēn tēn en nomō(i) genomenos amemptos (Phil. 3:6)," *JBL* 53 (1934): 257-67.

0372 Thomas R. Schreiner, "Paul and Perfect Obedience to the Law: An Evaluation of the View of E. P. Sanders," *WTJ* 47 (1985): 245-78.

3:7-16

0373 J. T. Forestell, "Christian Perfection and Gnosis in Philippians 3,7-16," *CBQ* 15 (1953): 163-207.

3:7-15

0374 Ellen L. Babinsky, "Philippians 3:7-15," *Int* 49 (1995): 70-72.

3:7-14

0375 R. Bultmann, "Philipper 3:7-14," in *Marburger Predigten*. Tübingen: Mohr, 1956. Pp. 41-47.

3:7-9

0376 Pierre Bonnard, "Conversation biblique avec Jean Delumeau," *FV* 84 (1985): 77-81.

3:8-14

0377 G. Gaide, "C'est dans le Christ que nous nous glorifions," *AsSeign* N.S. 18 (1970): 48-54.

0378 A. Viard, "Le salut et la connaissance du Christ Jésus," *EV* 83 (1983): 78-79.

3:8-12

0379 D. M. Stanley, "The Apostle Paul as Saint," *SM* 35 (1986): 71-97.

3:8-9

0380 Mark R. Shaw, "Is There Salvation outside the Christian Faith," *EAJT* 2 (1983): 42-62.

3:8

0381 D. H. C. Read, "And the Winner is... the Star of the Saint," *ET* 90 (1978): 46-47.

3:9

0382 Mark A. Seifrid, "Paul's Approach to the Old Testament in Romans 10:6-8," *TriJ* N.S. 6 (1985): 3-37.

0383 James D. G. Dunn, "Once More, Pistis Christou," *SBLSP* 30 (1991): 730-44.

3:10-16

0384 G. T. Montague, "Transformation in Christ and the Race for the Prize," in *Growth in Christ*. Kirwood: Maryhurst Press, 1961. Pp. 122-35.

3:10-11

0385 P. Joüon, "Notes philologiques sur quelques versets de l'épître aux Philippiens," *RechSR* 28 (1948): 88-93, 299-310.

0386 D. M. Stanley, "Christ's Resurrection: A Force in the Christian Life. Phil. 3, 10-11)," in *Christ's Resurrection in Pauline Soteriology*. Rome: Pontifical Biblical Institute, 1961. Pp. 102-105.

0387 Richard D. Patterson, "Attaining to the Resurrection," *FundJ* 4 (1985): 53.

0388 Andrew C. Perriman, "The Pattern of Christ's Sufferings: Colossians 1:24 and Philippians 3:10-11," *TynB* 42 (1991): 62-79.

3:10

0389 B. Ahern, "The Fellowship of His Sufferings," *CBQ* 22 (1960): 1-32.

0390 Joseph A. Fitzmyer, "To Know Him and the Power of His Resurrection (Philippians 3:10)," in A.-L. Descamps and André Halleux, eds., *Mélanges bibliques en hommage au R. P. Béda Rigaux*. Gembloux: Duculot, 1970. Pp. 411-25.

0391 Leopold Sabourin, "Koinonia in the New Testament," *RSB* 1 (1981): 109-15.

0392 Christian Wolff, "Niedrigkeit und Verzicht in Wort und Weg Jesu und in der apostolischen Existenz des Paulus," *NTS* 34 (1988): 183-96.

0393 Michael Wolter, "Der Apostel und seine Gemeinden als Teilhaber am Leidensgeschick Jesu Christi: Beobachtungen zur paulinischen Leidenstheologie," *NTS* 36 (1990): 535-57.

3:11

0394 Donald L. Norbie, "If by Any Means," *EQ* 32 (1960): 224-26.

0395 I. Peri, "Gelangen zur Vollkommenheit: Zur Lateinischen Interpretation von Katantao in Eph 4:13," *BZ* 23/2 (1979): 269-78.

0396   J. Terry Young, "Resurrection Theology," *BI* 14/1 (1987): 65-67.

0397   Randall E. Otto, " 'If Possible I May Attain the Resurrection from the
            Dead'," *CBQ* 57 (1995): 324-40.

3:12-21

0398   Wendell R. Debner, "Christ and the Church: The Ministry of the
            Baptized," *WW* 7 (1987): 417-23.

3:12-15

0399   R.-H. Esnault, "Philippians 3:12-15," *ETR* 30 (1955): 22-26.

3:12-14

0400   G. S. Gibson, "A Divine Discontent," *ET* 94 (1983): 372-73.

0401   François Refoulé, "Note sur Romains 9:30-33," *RB* 92 (1985):
            161-86.

3:12

0402   E. Lopez, "En torno a Fil 3,12," *EB* 34 (1975) 121-23.

0403   Karl H. Schelkle, "Im Leib oder Ausser des Leibes: Paulus als
            Mystiker," in William C. Weinrich, ed., *The New Testament Age*
            (festschrift for Bo Reicke). 2 vols. Macon GA: Mercer Universitry
            Press, 1984. Pp. 455-65.

3:13-14

0404   Anne-Marie La Bonnardière, "Les deux vies: Marthe et Marie (Luc
            10,38-42)," in Anne-Marie La Bonnardière, ed., *Saint Augustin et la
            Bible*. Paris: Editions Beauchesne, 1986. Pp. 411-25.

0405   Denis M. Farkasfalvy, "The Use of Paul by Bernard as Illustrated by
            Saint Bernard's Interpretation of Philippians 3:13," in John R.
            Sommerfeldt, ed., *Bernardus Magister: Papers Presented at the
            Nonacentenary Celebration of the Birth of Saint Bernard of
            Clairvaux*. Kalamazoo MI: Cistercian Publications, 1992. Pp. 161-68.

3:15

0406   P. Joüon, "Notes philologiques sur quelques versets de l'épître aux
            Philippiens," *RechSR* 28 (1948): 88-93, 299-310.

3:17-4:3

0407   F. Ogara, "Nostra conversatio in caelis est," *VD* 18 (1948): 321-28.

0408 B. Trémel, "La voie de la perfection chrétienne," *AsSeign* 78 (1965): 17-24.

3:17-4:1

0409 B. Trémel, "La voie de la perfection chrétienne," *AsSeign* N.S. 15 (1973): 37-42.

0410 Ulrich B. Müller, "Prophetische Gerichtspredigt bei Paulus," in *Prophetie und Predigt im Neuen Testament*. Gütersloh: Mohn, 1975. Pp. 175-214.

0411 A. Viard, "Tenez bon dans le Seigneur," *EV* 83 (1983): 55-56.

3:17-21

0412 Wendy Cotter, "Our politeuma Is in Heaven: The Meaning of Philippians 3:17-21," in Bradley H. McLean, ed., *Origins and Method: Towards a New Understanding of Judaism and Christianity* (festschrift for John C. Hurd). Sheffield UK: JSOT Press, 1993. Pp. 92-104.

3:17

0413 P. Joüon, "Notes philologiques sur quelques versets de l'épître aux Philippiens," *RechSR* 28 (1948): 88-93, 299-310.

0414 F. Wulf, "Seid meine Nachahmer, Brüder!" *GeistL* 34 (1961): 241-47.

0415 D. M. Stanley, "Imitation in Paul's Letters: Its Significance for His Relationship to Jesus and to His Own Christian Foundations," in Peter Richardson and John C. Hurd, eds., *From Jesus to Paul* (festschrift for Francis W. Beare). Waterloo: Wilfrid Laurier University Press, 1984. Pp. 127-41.

0416 Otto Merk, "Nachahmung Christi: zu ethischen Perspektiven in der paulinischen Theologie," in Helmut Merklein, ed., *Neues Testament und Ethik* (festschrift for Rudolf Schnackenburg). Freiburg: Herder, 1989. Pp. 172-206.

3:18

0417 Daniel B. Wallace, "The Semantics and Exegetical Significance of the Object-Complement Construction in the New Testament," *GTJ* 6 (1985): 91-112.

3:19

0418   P. Joüon, "Notes philologiques sur quelques versets de l'épître aux Philippiens," *RechSR* 28 (1948): 88-93, 299-310.

0419   Mark A. Seifrid, "Paul's Approach to the Old Testament in Romans 10:6-8," *TriJ* N.S. 6 (1985): 3-37.

0420   J. Moiser, "The Meaning of *koilia* in Philippians 3:19," *ET* 108 (1998): 365-66.

3:20-21

0421   N. Flanagan, "A Note on Philippians 3,20-21," *CBQ* 18 (1956): 8-9.

0422   D. M. Stanley, "The Christian Eschatological Hope of Salvation. Phil. 3, 20-21)," in *Christ's Resurrection in Pauline Soteriology.* Rome: Pontifical Biblical Institute, 1961. Pp. 105-107.

0423   E. Güttgemanns, "Die Problematik von Phil. 3:20f.," in *Der leidende Apostel und sein Herr.* Göttingen: Vandenhoeck & Ruprecht, 1966. Pp. 240-47.

0424   Jürgen Becker, "Erwägungen zu Phil 3:20-21," *TZ* 27 (1971): 16-29.

0425   John Reumann, "Philippians 3:20-21 - A Hymnic Fragment?" *NTS* 30 (1984): 593-609.

0426   Jürgen Becker, "Paulus und seine Gemeinden," in Jürgen Becker, et al., eds., *Die Anfänge des Christentums: alte Welt und neue Hoffnung.* Stuttgart: W. Kohlhammer, 1987. Pp. 102-59.

0427   Per Bilde, "Eskatologi, soteriologi og kosmologi hos Paulus på grundlag af Fil.3,20-21 og beslægtede tekster: Et bidrag til debatten om Gronbechs Paulus-bog," *DTT* 54 (1991): 209-27.

3:20

0428   Paul C. Böttger, "Die eschatologische Existenz der Christen: Erwägungen zu Philipper 3:20," *ZNW* 60 (1969): 244-63.

0429   K. Aland, "Die Christen und der Staat nach Phil. 3,20," in *Paganisme, Judaïsme, Christianisme: Influences et affrontements dans le monde antique* (festschrift for Marcel Simon). Paris: De Boccard, 1978. Pp. 247-59.

0430 Michael R. Austin, "Salvation and the Divinity of Jesus," *ET* 96 (1985): 271-75.

0431 Gary Hardin, "A Theology of Heaven," *BI* 14/1 (1987): 18-21.

3:21

0432 Gedaliahu A. G. Stroumsa, "Form(s) of God: Some Notes on Metatron and Christ," *HTR* 76 (1983): 269-88.

0433 Michael B. Dick, "Conversion in the Bible," in Robert D. Duggan, ed., *Conversion and the Catechumenate.* Ramsey NJ: Paulist Press, 1984. Pp. 43-63.

0434 Larry W. Hurtado, "Jesus as Lordly Example in Philippians 2:5-11," in Peter Richardson and John C. Hurd, eds., *From Jesus to Paul* (festschrift for Francis W. Beare). Waterloo: Wilfrid Laurier University Press, 1984. Pp. 113-26.

0435 Eugene F. Klug, "The Doctrine of Man: Christian Anthropology," *CTQ* 48 (1984): 141-52.

0436 Luis F. Landaria, "Eucaristía y escatología," *EE* 59 (1984): 211-16.

0437 John S. Pobee, "Human Transformation: A Biblical View," *MS* 2 (1985): 5-9.

0438 Jean Doignon, "Comment Hilaire de Poitiers a-t-il lu et compris le verset de Paul, Philippiens 3:21?" *VC* 43 (1989): 127-37.

4:1-20

0439 A. H. Snyman, "Persuasion in Philippians 4:1-20," in Stanley E. Porter, and Thomas H. lbricht, eds., *Rhetoric and the New Testament.* Sheffield UK: JSOT Press, 1993. Pp. 325-37.

4:1

0440 Ceslaus Spicq, "ἐπιποθεῖν désirer ou chérir?" *RB* 64 (1957): 184-95.

0441 Derek Thomas, "Standing Firm! Philippians 4:1," *Evangel* 11 (1993): 39-43.

4:2-23

0442 C. H. Giblin, "Closing Sentiments of Peace and Joy," in *In Hope of God's Glory.* New York: Herder and Herder, 1970. Pp. 117-20.

4:2-3

0443 M. Adinolfi, "Le collaboratrici ministeriali di Paolo nelle lettere ai Romani e ai Filippesi," *BibO* 17 (1975): 21-32.

0444 Francis X. Malinowski, "The Brave Women of Philippi," *BTB* 15 (1985): 60-64.

0445 Nils A. Dahl, "Euodia and Syntyche and Paul's Letter to the Philippians," in L. Michael White and O. Larry Yarbrough, eds., *The Social World of the First Christians* (festschrift for Wayne A. Meeks). Minneapolis: Fortress Press, 1995. Pp. 3-15.

4:2

0446 Wendy Cotter, "Women's Authority Roles in Paul's Churches: Countercultural or Conventional?" *NovT* 36 (1994): 350-72.

4:3

0447 Milan Hájek, "Comments on Philippians 4:3 - Who Was 'gnésios syzygos'?" *CVia* 7 (1964): 261-62.

0448 Charles R. Smith, "The Book of Life," *GTJ* 6 (1985): 219-30.

0449 G. W. Murray, "Paul's Corporate Witness in Philippians," *BSac* 155 (1998): 316-26.

4:4-20

0450 Carl Loeliger, "Biblical Concepts of Salvation," *Point* 6 (1977): 134-45.

4:4-13

0451 Charles B. Bugg, "Philippians 4:4-13," *RevExp* 88 (1991): 253-57.

4:4-9

0452 P. Dacquino, "La gioia cristiana," *BibO* 3 (1961): 182-83.

4:4-7

0453 G. Gaide, "La joie et la paix dans le Seigneur," *AsSeign* 5 (1966): 32-40.

0454 A. Sisti, "Gioia e pace," *BibO* 8 (1966): 263-72.

0455 G. Gaide, "Joie et paix dans le Seigneur," *AsSeign* N.S. 7 (1969): 59-64.

0456 J. Sudbrack, "Mut zur Freude! Paulus an die Gemeinde von Philippi," *GeistL* 43 (1970): 81-86.

0457 Helmut Tacke, "Verheissung in den Predigtmeditationen Hans Joachim Iwands," in Hans-Georg Geyer, et al., eds., *"Wenn nicht jetzt, wann dann"* (festschrift for Hans-Joachim Kraus). Neukirchen-Vluyn: Neukirchener Verlag, 1983. Pp. 395-404.

4:4

0458 T. Camelot, "Réjouissez-vous dans le Seigneur toujours," *VS* 89 (1953): 474-81.

0459 Will K. Morris, "Rejoice Always," *ChrM* 16 (1985): 24.

4:5

0460 Allan Chapple, " 'The Lord Is Near'," in David Peterson John Pryor, eds., *In the Fullness of Time* (festschrift for Donald Robinson). Homebush West NSW: Lancer, 1992. Pp. 149-65.

4:6-9

0461 C. Bigaré, "La paix de Dieu dans le Christ Jésus," *AsSeign* N.S. 58 (1974): 11-15.

4:6-7

0462 J. S. Stewart, "Old Texts in Modern Translation: Philippians 4:6-7," *ET* 49 (1937-1938): 269-71.

0463 Kenneth S. Kantzer, "Disturbing the Peace: Born This Day in the City of David a Tough-Minded Peacemaker," *CT* 29 (1985): 18.

4:6

0464 G. P. Wiles, "Philippians 4:6," in *Paul's Intercessory Prayers: The Significance of the Intercessory Prayer Passages in the Letters of St. Paul.* Cambridge: University Press, 1974. Pp. 286-89.

0465 A. M. Hunter, "The Magnanimity of Christ," in *Gospel and Apostle.* London: SCM Press, 1975. Pp. 44-47.

4:7

0466 M. Zerwick, "Gaudium et pax custodia cordium," *VD* 31 (1953): 101-104.

0467 J. Walsh, "The Peace that Passes Understanding," *Way* 22 (1982): 27-39.

4:8-9

0468 James Gaderlund, "To Stand Firm in the Lord," *CQ* 43 (1985): 21-25.

0469 P. A. Holloway, *"Bona Cogitarea*: An Epicurean Consolation in Philippians 4:8-9," *HTR* 91 (1998): 89-96.

4:10-20

0470 Otto Glombitza, "Der Dank des Apostels: zum Verständnis von Philipper 4:10-20," *NovT* 7 (1964): 135-41.

0471 Pheme Perkins, "Christology, Friendship and Status: The Rhetoric of Philippians," *SBLSP* 26 (1987): 509-20.

0472 Gerald W. Peterman, "Thankless Thanks: The Epistolary Social Convention in Philippians 4:10-20," *TynB* 42 (1991): 261-70.

0473 Ken L. Berry, "The Function of Friendship Language in Philippians 4:10-20," in John T. Fitzgerald, ed., *Friendship, Flattery, and Frankness of Speech: Studies on Friendship in the New Testament World*. Leiden: E. J. Brill, 1996. Pp. 107-24

4:10

0474 Norbert Baumert, "1st Philipper 4:10 richtig übersetzt?" *BZ* N.S. 13 (1969): 256-62.

4:11

0475 G. Priero, "Didici sufficiens esse," *RivBib* 10 (1962): 59-63.

0476 Abraham J. Malherbe, "Paul's Self-Sufficiency," in John T. Fitzgerald, ed., *Friendship, Flattery, and Frankness of Speech: Studies on Friendship in the New Testament W/rld*. Leiden: E. J. Brill, 1996. Pp. 125-39.

4:12-20

0477 B. Rolland, "Saint Paul et la pauvreté," *AsSeign* N.S. 59 (1974): 10-15.

4:12

0478 Larry W. Hurtado, "Jesus as Lordly Example in Philippians 2:5-11," in Peter Richardson and John C. Hurd, eds., *From Jesus to Paul* (festschrift for Francis W. Beare). Waterloo: Wilfrid Laurier University Press, 1984. Pp. 113-26.

4:15-16

0479 William R. Herzog, "The New Testament and the Question of Racial Injustice," *ABQ* 5 (1986): 12-32.

4:16

0480 L. Morris, "Kai apaks kai dis," *NovT* 1 (1956): 205-208.

0481 Roger L. Omanson, "Translations: Text and Interpretation," *EQ* 57 (1985): 195-210.

0482 Gerald L. Borchert, "Thessalonica," *BI* 14/1 (1987): 62-64.

4:18-19

0483 P. Joüon, "Notes philologiques sur quelques versets de l'épître aux Philippiens," *RechSR* 28 (1948): 88-93, 299-310.

4:18

0484 R. Corriveau, *The Liturgy of Life: A Study of the Ethical Thought of St. Paul in His Letters to the Early Christian Communities*. Paris: Desclée de Brouwer, 1970. Pp. 111-17.

0485 David G. Peterson, "Further Reflections on Worship in the New Testament," *RTR* 44 (1985): 34-41.

4:19

0486 H.-M. Dion, "La notion paulinienne de "richesse de Dieu' et ses sources," *SE* 18 (1966): 139-48.

4:21

0487 G. W. Murray, "Paul's Corporate Witness in Philippians," *BSac* 155 (1998): 316-26.

4:22

0488 Peter Lampe, "Iunia-Iunias: Sklavenherkunft im Kreise der vorpaulischen Apostel," *ZNW* 76 (1985): 132-34.

PART TWO

Citations by Subjects

anthropology
0489 Eugene F. Klug, "The Doctrine of Man: Christian Anthropology," *CTQ* 48 (1984): 141-52.

anthropomorphism
0490 Gedaliahu A. G. Stroumsa, "Form(s) of God: Some Notes on Metatron and Christ," *HTR* 76 (1983): 269-88.

apocalyptic literature
0491 Andrew Chester, "Jewish Messianic Expectations and Mediatorial Figures and Pauline Christology," in Martin Hengel and Ulrich Heckel, eds., *Paulus und das antike Judentum* (festschrift for Adolf Schlatter). Tübingen: Mohr, 1991. Pp. 17-89.

ascension
0492 Paul Trudinger, "Making Sense of the Ascension: The Cross as Glorification," *SMR* 133 (1988): 11-13.

atonement
0493 Christophe Senft, "Paul et Jésus," *FV* 84 (1985): 49-56.

baptism
0494 Stephen W. Sykes, "The Strange Persistence of Kenotic Christology," in Alistair Kee and Eugene T. Long, eds., *Being and Truth* (festschrift for John Macquarrie). London: SCM Press, 1986. Pp. 349-75.

Chiasmus
0495 John Breck, "Biblical chiasmus: Exploring Structure for Meaning," *BTB* 17 (1987): 70-74.

Christology
0496 Charles M. Horne, "Let This Mind Be in You," *JETS* 3 (1960): 37-44.

0497 P. A. van Stempvoort, "De betekenis van Filippenzen 2:5 t/m 11," *NTT* 19 (1964): 97-111.

0498 Joseph Coppens, "Phil 2:7 et Is 53:12, le problème de la 'kénose'," *ETL* 41 (1965): 147-50.

0499 André Feuillet, "L'hymne christologique de l'Epitre aux Philippiens 2:6-11," *RB* 72 (1965): 352-80.

0500 David H. Wallace, "Note on Morphe," *TZ* 22 (1966): 19-25.

0501 Joseph Coppens, "Une nouvelle structuration de l'hymne christologique de l'Epître aux Philippiens," *ETL* 43 (1967): 197-202.

0502 Charles H. Talbert, "Problem of Pre-existence in Philippians 2:6-11," *JBL* 86 (1967): 141-53.

0503 Norman K. Bakken, "New Humanity: Christ and the Modern Age," *Int* 22 (1968): 71-82.

0504 James A. Sanders, "Dissenting Deities and Philippians 2:1-11," *JBL* 88 (1969): 279-90.

0505 John G. Gibbs, "Relation between Creation and Redemption according to Philippians 2:5-11," *NovT* 12 (1970): 270-83.

0506 Jürgen Becker, "Erwägungen zu Phil 3:20-21," *TZ* 27 (1971): 16-29.

0507 Ulrich Browarzik, "Die dogmatische Frage nach der Göttlichkeit Jesu," *NZSTR* 13 (1971): 164-75.

0508 Thomas F. Glasson, "Two notes on the Philippians hymn 2:6-11," *NTS* 21 (1974): 133-39.

0509 Bruno Corsani, "Gesù Cristo è il Signore," in Maria Vingiani, et al., eds., *Ecumenismo oggi: bilancio e prospettive: atti della XIII Sessione di formaziona ecumenica.* Turin: Elle Di Ci, 1975. Pp. 195-205.

0510 Jacobus T. Bakker, "De tweevoudige gerechtigheid: Luthers 'sermo de duplici Iustitia', 1518," in Jacobus T. Bakker and J. P. Boendermaker, eds., *Luther na 500 jaar: teksten, vertaald en besproken.* Kampen: Kok, 1983. Pp. 30-57.

0511 Norman K. Bakken, "Uma nova criaçao: o Cristo para o nosso tempo," *EstT* 24 (1984): 118-28.

0512 Larry W. Hurtado, "Jesus as Lordly Example in Philippians 2:5-11," in Peter Richardson and John C. Hurd, eds., *From Jesus to Paul* (festschrift for Francis W. Beare). Waterloo: Wilfrid Laurier University Press, 1984. Pp. 113-26.

0513 Byung-Mu Ahn, "The Body of Jesus-Event Tradition," *EAJT* 3 (1985): 293-309.

0514 Franz Mussner, "Das Reich Christi: Bemerkungen zur Eschatologie des Corpus Paulinum," in Michael Böhnke and Hanspeter Heinz, eds., *Im Gespräch mit dem dreieinen Gott: Elemente einer trinitarischen Theologie* (festschrift for Wilhelm Breuning). Düsseldorf: Patmos Verlag, 1985. Pp. 141-55.

0515 Ian G. Scott, "Jesus is Lord," *ET* 96 (1985): 305-307.

0516 Christophe Senft, "Paul et Jésus," *FV* 84 (1985): 49-56.

0517 L. D. Hurst, "Re-enter the Pre-existent Christ in Philippians 2:5-11," *NTS* 32 (1986): 449-57.

0518 Alphonse Maillot, "Les théologies de la mort du Christ chez Paul," *FV* 85 (1986): 33-45.

0519 Florence M. Gillman, "Another Look at Romans 8:3: 'In the Likeness of Sinful Flesh'," *CBQ* 49 (1987): 597-604.

0520 Pheme Perkins, "Christology, Friendship and Status: The Rhetoric of Philippians," *SBLSP* 26 (1987): 509-20.

0521 Charles A. Wanamaker, "Philippians 2:6-11: Son of God or Adamic Christology?" *NTS* 33 (1987): 179-93.

0522 Ulrich B. Müller, "Der Christushymnus Phil 2:6-11," *ZNW* 79 (1988): 17-44.

0523 Nikolaus Walter, "Geschichte und Mythos in der urchristlichen Präexistenzchristologie," in Hans H. Schmid, ed., *Mythos und Rationalität*. Gütersloh: Gütersloher Verlaghaus Mohn, 1988. Pp. 224-34.

0524 Michel Gourgues, "La foi chrétienne primitive face à la croix: le témoignage des formulaires pré-pauliniens," *ScE* 41 (1989): 49-69.

0525 Otto Merk, "Nachahmung Christi: zu ethischen Perspektiven in der paulinischen Theologie," in Helmut Merklein, ed., *Neues Testament und Ethik* (festschrift for Rudolf Schnackenburg). Freiburg: Herder, 1989. Pp. 172-206.

0526 Ulrich Schoenborn, "El yo y los demas en el discurso paulino," *RevB* 51 (1989): 163-80.

0527   Albert Verwilghen, "Le Christ médiateur selon Ph 2,6-7 dans l'oeuvre
        de saint Augustin," in Bernard Bruning, et al., eds., *Collectanea
        Augustiniana* (festshcrift for T. J. van Bavel). Volume 2. Louvain:
        Leuven University Press, 1990. Pp. 469-82.

0528   Andrew Chester, "Jewish Messianic Expectations and Mediatorial
        Figures and Pauline Christology," in Martin Hengel and Ulrich
        Heckel, eds., *Paulus und das antike Judentum* (festschrift for Adolf
        Schlatter). Tübingen: Mohr, 1991. Pp. 17-89.

0529   James D. G. Dunn, "Once More, Pistis Christou," *SBLSP* 30 (1991):
        730-44.

0530   George W. E. Nickelsburg, "The Incarnation: Paul's Solution to the
        Universal Human Predicament," in Birger Pearson, et al., eds., *The
        Future of Early Christianity* (festschrift for Helmut Koester).
        Minneapolis: Fortress Press, 1991. Pp. 348-57.

0531   Andrew C. Perriman, "The Pattern of Christ's Sufferings: Colossians
        1:24 and Philippians 3:10-11," *TynB* 42 (1991): 62-79.

0532   John Reumann, "Christology in Philippians," in Cilliers Breytenbach
        and Henning Paulsen, eds., *Anfänge der Christologie* (festschrift for
        Ferdinand Hahn). Göttingen: Vandenhoeck & Ruprecht, 1991. Pp.
        131-40.

0533   Alberto Viciano, "Aspects christologiques du 'Corpus Paulinum' dans
        la controverse antimanichéenne de Saint Augustin," in Alois van
        Tongerloo and Soren Giversen, eds., *Manichaica selecta* (festschrift
        for Julien Ries. Louvain: International Association of Manichaean
        Studies, 1991. Pp. 379-89.

0534   Hendrikus Boers and Donna Singles, trans. Louis Panier, "L'histoire
        de Jésus et le mythe du Christ," in Louis Panier, ed., *Le temps de la
        lecture: exégèse biblique et sémiotique* (festschrift for Jean Delorme).
        Paris, Cerf, 1993. Pp. 185-202

0535   Roland Bergmeier, "Weihnachten mit und ohne Glanz: Notizen zu
        Johannesprolog und Philipperhymnus," *ZNW* 85 (1994): 47-68.

0536   Enrique B. Triever, "S'en aller et être avec Christ (Philippiens 1/23),"
        ETR 69 (1994): 559-63.

0537 Gerald Bostock, "Origen's Exegesis of the Kenosis Hymn," in Gilles Dorival and Alain Le Boulluec, eds., *Origeniana sexta: Origène et la Bible*. Louvain: Peeters, 1995. Pp. 531-47.

0538 H. Navarro Cuervo, "La kénosis de Cristo," *May* 22 (1996): 339-436.

0539 Veronica Koperski, *The Knowledge of Christ Jesus My Lord: The High Christology of Philippians 3:7-11*. Kampen: Kok Pharos, 1996.

0540 Enrique Treiyer, "S'en aller et etre avec Christ: Philippiens 1:23," *AUSS* 34 (1996): 47-64.

0541 Ralph P. Martin and Brian J. Dodd, eds., *Where Christology Began: Essays on Philippians 2*. Louisville: Westminster/John Knox Press, 1998.

0542 A. J. McClain, "The Doctrine of the Kenosis in Philippians 2:5-8," *MSJ* 9 (1998): 85-96.

crucifixion

0543 Guy Wagner, "Le scandale de la croix expliqué par le chant du serviteur d'Esaïe 53: réflexion sur Philippiens 2:6-11," *ETR* 61 (1986): 177-87.

deacons

0544 George W. Knight, "Two Offices and Two Orders of Elders: A New Testament Study," *Pres* 11 (1985): 1-12.

death

0545 Anne Hetzel, "L'accompagnement des mourants," *FV* 84 (1985): 29-45.

0546 Günter Klein, "Aspekte ewigen Lebens im Neuen Testament: ein theologischer Annähungsversuch," *ZTK* 82 (1985): 48-70.

deutero-Pauline

0547 Darrell J. Doughty, "Citizens of Heaven: Philippians 3:2-21," *NTS* 41 (1995): 102-22.

early church

0548 A. F. J. Klijn, "Paul's Opponents in Philippians 3," *NovT* 7 (1965): 278-84.

ecclesiology
0549   J. Hainz, "Die Sorge des Apostels um seine Gemeinden und die Sorge
        der Gemeinden für ihren Apostel nach dem Brief an die Philipper," in
        *Ekklesia: Strukturen paulinischer Gemeinde-Theologie und
        Gemeinde-Ordnung.* Regensburg: Pustet, 1972. Pp. 21 0-26.

0550   Rolf Gögler, "Inkarnationsglaube und Bibeltheologie bei Origenes,"
        TQ 165 (1985): 82-94.

0551   Paul D. Hanson, "The Identity and Purpose of the Church," *TT* 42
        (1985): 342-52.

0552   Jean Marc Laporte, "Kenosis and koinonia: The Path Ahead for
        Anglican-Roman Catholic Dialogue," *OC* 21 (1985): 102-20.

0553   Roselyne Dupont-Roc, "De l'hymne christologique à une vie de
        koinonia: Etude sur la lettre aux Philippiens," *EB* 49 (1991): 451-72.

0554   Davorin Peterlin, *Paul's Letter to the Philippians in the Light of
        Disunity in the Church.* Leiden: E. J. Brill, 1995.

elders
0555   George W. Knight, "Two Offices and Two Orders of Elders: A New
        Testament Study," *Pres* 11 (1985): 1-12.

Epaphroditus
0556   Bernhard Mayer, "Paulus als Vermittler zwischen Epaphroditus und
        der Gemeinde von Philippi: Bemerkungen zu Phil 2:25-30," *BZ* N.S.
        31 (1987): 176-88.

eschatology
0557   James B. Hester, "The Reflections from Philippians That Evidence
        Paul's Eschatology," master's thesis, Southwestern Baptist
        Theological Seminary, Fort Worth TX, 1952.

0558   D. M. Stanley, "The Christian Eschatological Hope of Salvation. Phil.
        3, 20-21)," in *Christ's Resurrection in Pauline Soteriology.* Rome:
        Pontifical Biblical Institute, 1961. Pp. 105-107.

0559   Paul C. Böttger, "Die eschatologische Existenz der Christen:
        Erwägungen zu Philipper 3:20," *ZNW* 60 (1969): 244-63.

0560   Jürgen Becker, "Erwägungen zu Phil 3:20-21," *TZ* 27 (1971): 16-29.

0561 S. De Ausejo, "Es un himno a Cristo el prólogo de San Juan? Los himnos cristologicos de la Iglesia primitiva y el prólogo del IV Evangelio," in *La escatologia individual neotestamentana* a la luz de las ideas en los tiempos apostolicos. Madrid: Consejo Superior de Investigaciones Científicas, 1972. Pp. 307-96.

0562 J. M. Gonzalez Ruiz, "Las asambleas cultuales en las epístolas de la cautividad," in *La escatologia individual neotestamentana* a la luz de las ideas en los tiempos apostolicos. Madrid: Consejo Superior de Investigaciones Científicas, 1972. Pp. 291-306.

0563 P. Hoffmann, "Das Mit-Christus-Sein im Tode nach Phil 1, 21-26," in *Die Toten in Christus: Eine religionsgeschichtliche und exegetische Untersuchung zur paulinischen Eschatologie*. Münich: Aschendorff, 1972. Pp. 286-320.

0564 Luis F. Landaria, "Eucaristía y escatología," *EE* 59 (1984): 211-16.

0565 Michel Bouttier, "Petite suite paulinienne," *ETR* 60 (1985): 265-72.

0566 Günter Klein, "Aspekte ewigen Lebens im Neuen Testament: ein theologischer Annähungsversuch," *ZTK* 82 (1985): 48-70.

0567 Franz Mussner, "Das Reich Christi: Bemerkungen zur Eschatologie des Corpus Paulinum," in Michael Böhnke and Hanspeter Heinz, eds., *Im Gespräch mit dem dreieinen Gott: Elemente einer trinitarischen Theologie* (festschrift for Wilhelm Breuning). Düsseldorf: Patmos Verlag, 1985. Pp. 141-55.

0568 Thomas F. Dailey, "To Live or Die: Paul's Eschatological Dilemma in Philippians 1:19-26," *Int* 44 (1990): 18-28.

0569 Per Bilde, "Eskatologi, soteriologi og kosmologi hos Paulus på grundlag af Fil.3,20-21 og beslægtede tekster: Et bidrag til debatten om Gronbechs Paulus-bog," *DTT* 54 (1991): 209-27.

ethics

0570 Henk B. Kossen, "Der Friedensbegriff in der Bibel," in *Christen im Streit um den Frieden: Beiträge zu einer neuen Friedensethik*. Freiburg: Dreisam-Verlag, 1982. Pp. 36-47.

0571   Michael B. Dick, "Conversion in the Bible," in Robert D. Duggan, ed., *Conversion and the Catechumenate*. Ramsey NJ: Paulist Press, 1984. Pp. 43-63.

0572   D. M. Stanley, "Imitation in Paul's Letters: Its Significance for His Relationship to Jesus and to His Own Christian Foundations," in Peter Richardson and John C. Hurd, eds., *From Jesus to Paul* (festschrift for Francis W. Beare). Waterloo: Wilfrid Laurier University Press, 1984. Pp. 127-41.

0573   William S. Kurz, "Kenotic Imitation of Paul and of Christ in Philippians 2 and 3," in Fernando F. Segovia, ed., *Discipleship in the New Testament*. Philadelphia: Fortress Press, 1985. Pp. 103-26.

0574   William R. Herzog, "The New Testament and the Question of Racial Injustice," *ABQ* 5 (1986): 12-32.

0575   Albert Verwillghen, "Le Christ Jésus, source de l'humilité chrétienn (Phil 2,6-8)," in Anne-Marie La Bonnardière, ed., *Saint Augustin et la Bible*. Paris: Editions Beauchesne, 1986. Pp. 427-37.

0576   John B. Webster, "Christology, Imitability and Ethics," *SJT* 39 (1986): 309-26.

0577   John B. Webster, "The Imitation of Christ," *TynB* 37 (1986): 95-120.

0578   Jürgen Becker, "Paulus und seine Gemeinden," in Jürgen Becker, et al., eds., *Die Anfänge des Christentums: alte Welt und neue Hoffnung*. Stuttgart: W. Kohlhammer, 1987. Pp. 102-59.

0579   Michael Parsons, "Being Precedes Act: Indicative and Imperative in Paul's Writing," *EQ* 60 (1988): 99-127.

0580   Otto Merk, "Nachahmung Christi: zu ethischen Perspektiven in der paulinischen Theologie," in Helmut Merklein, ed., *Neues Testament und Ethik* (festschrift for Rudolf Schnackenburg). Freiburg: Herder, 1989. Pp. 172-206.

0581   L. Michael White, "Morality between Two Worlds: A Paradigm of Friendship in Philippians," in David L. Balch, et als., eds., *Greeks, Romans, and Christians* (festschrift for Abraham J. Malherbe). Minneapolis: Fortress Press, 1990. Pp. 201-15.

0582 Rodney R. Reeves, "To Be or Not to Be? That Is not the Question: Paul's Choice in Philippians 1:22," *PRS* 19 (1992): 273-89.

0583 Francis Young, "The Pastoral Epistles and the Ethics of Reading," *JSNT* 45 (1992): 105-20.

0584 James L. Jaquette, "Life and Death, Adiaphora, and Paul's Rhetorical Strategies," *NovT* 38 (1996): 30-54.

exaltation
0585 Paul Trudinger, "Making Sense of the Ascension: The Cross as Glorification," *SMR* 133 (1988): 11-13.

form criticism
0586 Georg Strecker, "Redaktion und Tradition im Christushymnus Phil 2:6-11," *ZNW* 55 (1964): 63-78.

0587 Byung-Mu Ahn, "The Body of Jesus-Event Tradition," *EAJT* 3 (1985): 293-309.

0588 David A. Black, "Paul and Christian Unity: A Formal Analysis of Philippians 2:1-4," *JETS* 28 (1985): 299-308.

0589 Edgar Haulotte, "Formation du corpus du Nouveau Testament: recherche d'un 'module' génératif intratextuel," in Christoph Theobald, ed., *Le canon des Ecritures: études historiques, exégétiques et systématiques*. Paris: Editions du Cerf, 1990. Pp. 255-439.

gentiles
0590 Thomas R. Schreiner, "Paul and Perfect Obedience to the Law: An Evaluation of the View of E. P. Sanders," *WTJ* 47 (1985): 245-78.

0591 Kenneth Grayston, "The Opponents in Philippians 3," *ET* 97 (1986): 170-72.

0592 Jürgen Becker, "Paulus und seine Gemeinden," in Jürgen Becker, et al., eds., *Die Anfänge des Christentums: alte Welt und neue Hoffnung*. Stuttgart: W. Kohlhammer, 1987. Pp. 102-59.

0593 Robert A. Wortham, "Christology as Community: Identity in the Philippians Hymn--The Philippians Hymn as Social Drama," *PRS* 23 (1996): 269-87.

gnosticism
  0594 Larry W. Hurtado, "Jesus as Lordly Example in Philippians 2:5-11,"
        in Peter Richardson and John C. Hurd, eds., *From Jesus to Paul*
        (festschrift for Francis W. Beare). Waterloo: Wilfrid Laurier
        University Press, 1984. Pp. 113-26.

grammar
  0595 William Schweer, "Aoristic Revelation in the Prison Epistles,"
        doctoral dissertation, Midwestern Baptist Theological Seminary,
        Kansas City KN, 1956.

  0596 Gene L. Munn, "A Grammatical and Syntactical Analysis of
        Philippians," doctoral dissertation, Southwestern Baptist Theological
        Seminary, Fort Worth TX, 1959.

Hellenist influence
  0597 Jürgen Becker, "Paulus und seine Gemeinden," in Jürgen Becker, et
        al., eds., *Die Anfänge des Christentums: alte Welt und neue
        Hoffnung*. Stuttgart: W. Kohlhammer, 1987. Pp. 102-59.

  0598 Heikki Räisänen, "Paul's Conversion and the Development of His
        View of the Law," *NTS* 33 (1987): 404-19.

  0599 Johnny Christensen, "Paulus livsfornaegteren? For og imod Vilhelm
        Gronbechs Paulustolkning," *DTT* 53 (1990): 1-18.

  0600 L. Michael White, "Morality between Two Worlds: A Paradigm of
        Friendship in Philippians," in David L. Balch, et als., eds., *Greeks,
        Romans, and Christians* (festschrift for Abraham J. Malherbe).
        Minneapolis: Fortress Press, 1990. Pp. 201-15.

  0601 Wendy Cotter, "Our politeuma Is in Heaven: The Meaning of
        Philippians 3:17-21," in Bradley H. McLean, ed., *Origins and
        Method: Towards a New Understanding of Judaism and Christianity*
        (festschrift for John C. Hurd). Sheffield UK: JSOT Press, 1993. Pp.
        92-104.

  0602 Samuel Vollenweider, "Die Waagschalen von Leben und Tod: Zum
        antiken Hintergrund von Phil 1,21-26," *ZNW* 85 (1994): 93-115.

Holy Spirit
  0603 Nicolas Ozoline, "Quelques images relatives à la célébration primitive
        de la cinquantaine pascale," in Achille M. Triacca and A. Pistoia, eds.,

L'église dans la liturgie. Rome: CLV - Edizioni Liturgiche, 1980. Pp. 231-53.

0604 Joseph R. Jeter "Sermons on the fruit of the Spirit," *Impact* 15 (1985): 1-64.

0605 Geevarghese Osthathios, "Conviction of Truth and Tolerance of Love," *IRM* 74 (1985): 490-96.

humility

0606 John G. Strelan, "Who Heals the Healers," *Point* 10 (1981): 170-79.

hymns

0607 Joseph Coppens, "Les affinités littéraires de l'hymne christologique Phil 2, 6-11," *ETL* 42 (1966): 238-41.

0608 Georg Strecker, "Redaktion und Tradition im Christushymnus Phil 2:6-11," *ZNW* 55 (1964): 63-78.

0609 Georg Strecker, "Zum Christushymnus in Phil 2," *TLZ* 89 (1964): 521-22.

0610 Lowell D. Streiker, "Christological Hymn in Philippians 2," *LQ* 16 (1964): 49-58.

0611 Joseph Coppens, "Phil 2:7 et Is 53:12, le problème de la 'kénose'," *ETL* 41 (1965): 147-50.

0612 André Feuillet, "L'hymne christologique de l'Epitre aux Philippiens 2:6-11," *RB* 72 (1965): 352-80.

0613 John Harvey, "New Look at the Christ Hymn in Philippians 2:6-11," *ET* 76 (1965): 337-39.

0614 Joseph Coppens, "Une nouvelle structuration de l'hymne christologique de l'Epître aux Philippiens," *ETL* 43 (1967): 197-202.

0615 Charles H. Talbert, "Problem of Pre-existence in Philippians 2:6-11," *JBL* 86 (1967): 141-53.

0616 Norman K. Bakken, "New Humanity: Christ and the Modern Age," *Int* 22 (1968): 71-82.

0617   I. Howard Marshall, "The Christ-Hymn in Philippians," *TynB* 19 (1968): 104-27.

0618   James A. Sanders, "Dissenting Deities and Philippians 2:1-11," *JBL* 88 (1969): 279-90.

0619   John G. Gibbs, "Relation between Creation and Redemption according to Philippians 2:5-11," *NovT* 12 (1970): 270-83.

0620   Bertold Klappert, "Arbeit Gottes und Mitarbeit des Menschen," in Jürgen Moltmann, ed., *Recht auf Arbeit, Sinn der Arbeit*. Münich: Kaiser Verlag, 1979. Pp. 84-134.

0621   Hans Becker and Reiner Kaczynski, eds., *Liturgie und Dichtung: Ein interdisziplinäres Kompendium, I: Historische Präsentation*. Sankt Ottilien: EOS Verlag, 1983.

0622   Larry W. Hurtado, "Jesus as Lordly Example in Philippians 2:5-11," in Peter Richardson and John C. Hurd, eds., *From Jesus to Paul* (festschrift for Francis W. Beare). Waterloo: Wilfrid Laurier University Press, 1984. Pp. 113-26.

0623   John Reumann, "Philippians 3:20-21 - A Hymnic Fragment?" *NTS* 30 (1984): 593-609.

0624   David A. Black, "Paul and Christian Unity: A Formal Analysis of Philippians 2:1-4," *JETS* 28 (1985): 299-308.

0625   Teresia Yai-Chow Wong, "The Problem of Pre-existence in Philippians 2:6-11," *ETL* 62 (1986): 267-82.

0626   Florence M. Gillman, "Another Look at Romans 8:3: 'In the Likeness of Sinful Flesh'," *CBQ* 49 (1987): 597-604.

0627   Pheme Perkins, "Christology, Friendship and Status: The Rhetoric of Philippians," *SBLSP* 26 (1987): 509-20.

0628   Mathias Rissi, "Der Christushymnus in Phil 2,6-11," in Wolfgang Haase, ed., *Principat 25, 4: Religion*. New York: Walter de Gruyter, 1987. Pp. 3315-26.

0629   David A. Black, "The Authorship of Philippians 2:6-11: Some Literary-Critical Observations," *CTR* 2 (1988): 269-89.

0630 Ulrich B. Müller, "Der Christushymnus Phil 2:6-11," *ZNW* 79 (1988): 17-44.

0631 François Rousseau, "Une disposition des versets de Philippiens 2:5-11," *SR* 17 (1988): 191-98.

0632 Mark A. Filbert, "An Analysis of 'All Praise to Thee, for Thou, O King Divine' and 'At the Name of Jesus' in Relation to Philippians 2:6-11," *Hymn* 40 (1989): 12-15.

0633 Edgar Haulotte, "Formation du corpus du Nouveau Testament: recherche d'un 'module' génératif intratextuel," in Christoph Theobald, ed., *Le canon des Ecritures: études historiques, exégétiques et systématiques*. Paris: Editions du Cerf, 1990. Pp. 255-439.

0634 Roselyne Dupont-Roc, "De l'hymne christologique à une vie de koinonia: Etude sur la lettre aux Philippiens," *EB* 49 (1991): 451-72.

0635 Steven J. Kraftchick, "A Necessary Detour: Paul's Metaphorical Understanding of the Philippian Hymn," *HBT* 15 (1993): 1-37.

0636 Markus Bockmuehl, " 'The Form of God': Variations on a Theme of Jewish Mysticism," *JTS* N.S. 48 (1997): 1-23.

inspiration
0637 Rolf Gögler, "Inkarnationsglaube und Bibeltheologie bei Origenes," *TQ* 165 (1985): 82-94.

introduction
0638 Paul Feine, *Die Abfassung des Philipperbriefes in Ephesus*. Gütersloh: C. Bertelsmann, 1916.

0639 G. S. Duncan, "A New Setting for St. Paul's Epistle to the Philippians," *ET* 43 (1931-1932): 7-11.

0640 C. J. Cadoux, "The Dates and Provenance of the Imprisonment Epistles of St. Paul," *ET* 45 (1933-1934): 471-73.

0641 J. M. Shaw, "The Message of the Epistles - Philippians," *ET* 45 (1933-1934): 203-209.

0642   G. S. Duncan, "The Epistles of the Imprisonment in Recent Discussion," *ET* 46 (1934-1935): 293-98.

0643   T. W. Manson, *St. Paul in Ephesus: The date of the Epistle to the Philippians*. Manchester: The Manchester University Press, 1939.

0644   E. C. Sheehan, "The Characteristic Uses of the Aorist Tense in Philippians," master's thesis, New Orleans Baptist Theological Seminary, New Orleans LA, 1943.

0645   H. Wedell, "Is the Term 'Captivity Epistles' Justified?" *Theology* 50 (1947): 366-72.

0646   A. C. Cotter, "The Epistles of the Captivity," *CBQ*, 11 (1949): 370-80.

0647   John E. Jones, "A Commentary on the Epistle of Paul to Philemon," doctoral dissertation, Southern Baptist Theological Seminary, Louisville KY, 1949.

0648   John H. Pickford, *Paul's Spiritual Autobiography*. London: Marshall, Morgan & Scott, 1949.

0649   Lewis A. Curtis, "An Investigation of the Philippians Problem," doctoral dissertation, New Orleans Baptist Theological Seminary, New Orleans LA, 1953.

0650   Jan D. Plenter, *De blijdschap in Paulus' brieven : een studie met diens brief aan de filippenzen als uitgangspunt*. Assen: Van Gorcum & Comp. N.V., 1953.

0651   G. S. Duncan, "Important Hypotheses Reconsidered-VI, Were Paul's Imprisonment Epistles Written from Ephesus?" *ET* 67 (1955-1956): 163-66.

0652   J. M. Furness, "The Authorship of Philippians ii. 6-11," *ET* 70 (1959-1960): 240-43.

0653   B. D. Rahtjen, "The Three Letters of Paul to the Philippians ," *NTS* 6 (1959-1960): 167-73.

0654   B. S. MacKay, "Further Thoughts on Philippians," *NTS* 7 (1960-1961): 161-70.

0655 D. M. Stanley, "Letters Written from Ephesus: Philippians, First Corinthians," in *Christ's Resurrection in Pauline Sotenology*. Rome: Pontifical Biblical Istitute, 1961. Pp. 94-127.

0656 G. Bornkamm, "Der Philipperbrief als paulinische Briefsammlung," in *Neotestamentica et Patristica* (festschrift for Oscar Cullmann). Leiden: Brill, 1962. Pp. 192-202.

0657 T. E. Pollard, "The Integrity of Philippians," *NTS* 13 (1966-1967): 57-66.

0658 P. Dacquino,"La lettera ai Filippesi," in *Il messaggio della salvezza*. 5 volumes. Elle Dici: Torino-Leumann, 1966-1970. 5:651-72.

0659 R. Jewett, "Conflicting Movements in the Early Church as Reflected in Philippians," *NovT* 12 (1970): 362-90.

0660 R. Jewett, "The Epistolary Thanksgiving and the Integrity of Philippians," *NovT* (1970): 40-53.

0661 G. Bornkamm, "Der Philipperbrief als paulinische Briefsammiung," in *Geschichte and Glaube: Gesammelte Aufsätze*. Münich: Kaiser. 1971. Pp. 195-205.

0662 J. Ferguson, "Philippians, John and the Traditions of Ephesus," *ET* (1971-1972): 85-87.

0663 A. M. Hunter, "Paul the Saint (Philippians)," in *Gospel and Apostle*. London: SCM Press, 1975. Pp. 154-58.

0664 W. J. Dalton, "The Integrity of Philippians, *Bib* 60 (1979): 97-102.

0665 D. Cook, "Stephanus Le Moyne and the Dissection of Philippians," *JTS* 32 (1981): 138-42.

0666 David E. Garland, "The Composition and Unity of Philippians: Some Neglected Literary Factors," *NovT* 27 (1985): 141-73.

0667 Daniel B. Wallace, "The Semantics and Exegetical Significance of the Object-Complement Construction in the New Testament," *GTJ* 6 (1985): 91-112.

0668   David A. Black, "The Authorship of Philippians 2:6-11: Some Literary-Critical Observations," *CTR* 2 (1988): 269-89.

0669   Karl P. Donfried and I. Howard Marshall, *The Theology of the Shorter Pauline Letters*. Cambridge: Cambridge University Press, 1993.

0670   Joseph A. Fitzmyer, "The Aramaic Background of Philippians 2:6-11," *CBQ* 50 (1988): 470-83.

0671   Tonneke Bijker, *Meer vreugde dan u denkt: de brief aan de christenen in Filippi*. Kampen: Kok, 1991.

0672   Lukas Bormann, *Philippi: Stadt und Christengemeinde zur Zeit des Paulus*. Leiden: E. J. Brill, 1995.

0673   Kenneth E. Bailey, " 'Inverted Parallelisms' and 'Encased Parables' in Isaiah and Their Significance for Old and New Testament Translation and Interpretation," in L. J. de Regt, et al., eds., *Literary Structure and Rhetorical Strategies in the Hebrew Bible*. Winona Lake IN: Eisenbrauns, 1996. Pp. 14-30.

0674   John Banker, *A Semantic and Structural Analysis of Philippians*. Dallas: Summer Institute of Linguistics, 1996.

0675   La Tanunya M. Bynum, *Paul's Prison Letters*. Elgin IL: Brethren Press, 1996.

0676   Ralph Brucker, *'Christushymnen' oder 'epideiktische Passagen'?: Studien zum Stilwechsel im Neuen Testament und seiner Umwelt*. Göttingen: Vandenhoeck & Ruprecht, 1997.

0677   Jonas Holmstrand, *Markers and Meaning in Paul: An Analysis of 1 Thessalonians, Philippians and Galatians*. Stockholm, Sweden: Almqvist & Wiksell International, 1997.

0678   Stanley E. Porter and Thomas H. Olbricht, eds., *The Rhetorical Analysis of Scripture: Essays from the 1995 London Conference*. Sheffield: Sheffield Academic Press, 1997.

0679   Jeffrey T. Reed, *A Discourse Analysis of Philippians: Method and Rhetoric in the Debate over Literary Integrity*. Sheffield: Sheffield Academic Press, 1997.

0680 Cynthia B. Kittredge, *Community and Authority: The Rhetoric of Obedience in the Pauline Tradition.* Harrisburg PA: Trinity Press International, 1998.

0681 Casey W. Davis, *Oral Bbiblical Ccriticism: The Influence of the Principles of Orality on the Literary Structure of Paul's Epistle to the Philippians.* Sheffield: Sheffield Academic Press, 1999.

0682 Stanley E. Porter and Jeffrey T. Reed, "Philippians as a Macro-Chiasm and Its Exegetical Significance," *NTS* 44 (1999): 213-31.

joy

0683 Will K. Morris, "Rejoice Always," *ChrM* 16 (1985): 24.

Judaziers
0684 Kenneth Grayston, "The Opponents in Philippians 3," *ET* 97 (1986): 170-72.

judgment
0685 Alvin L. Baker, "Eternal Security Rightly Understood," *FundJ* 3 (1984): 18-20.

justice
0686 Jacobus T. Bakker, "De tweevoudige gerechtigheid: Luthers 'sermo de duplici Iustitia', 1518," in Jacobus T. Bakker and J. P. Boendermaker, eds., *Luther na 500 jaar: teksten, vertaald en besproken.* Kampen: Kok, 1983. Pp. 30-57.

justification
0687 Anthony Hoekema, "How We See Ourselves," *CT* 29 (1985): 36-38.

0688 John Reumann, "Justification and the imitatio motif in Philippians," in George H. Anderson and James R. Crumley, eds., *Promoting Unity: Themes in Lutheran-Catholic Dialogue* (festschrift for Johannes Cardinal Willebrands). Minneapolis: Augsburg Fortress, 1989. Pp. 17-28.

kenosis
0689 R. Deichgräber, "Philipper 2,6-11," in *Gotteshymnus und Christushhymnus in der frühen Christenheit.* Pp. 118-33.

0690 F. Ogara, "Hoc sentite in vobis, quod et in Christo Iesu," *VD* 15 (1935): 99-109.

0691 A. A. Stephenson, "Christ's Self-abasement," *CBQ* 1 (1939): 296-313.

0692 Rufus R. Crozier, "The 'Kenosis' in a Christology," doctoral dissertation, Midwestern Baptist Theological Seminary, Kansas City KN, 1940.

0693 André Feuillet, "L'Homme-Dieu considéré dans sa condition terrestre," *RB* 51 (1942): 58-79.

0694 A. Ehrhardt "Jesus Christ and Alexander the Great," *JTS* 46 (1945): 45-51.

0695 V. Larrañaga, "El nombre sobre todo nombre dado a Jesús desde su Resurrección gloriosa," *EB* 6 (1947): 287-305.

0696 A. Ehrhardt, "Ein antikes Herrscherideal," *EvT* 8 (1948-1949): 101-10.

0697 J. Dupont, "Jésus-Christ dans son abaissement et son exaltation, d'après Phil., 2,6-11," *RechSR* 37 (1950): 500-14.

0698 L. Bouyer, " Arpagmos," in *Mélanges Jules Lebreton, RechSR* 39 (1951): 281-88.

0699 M. Meinertz, "Zum Verständnis des Christushymnus Phil. 2,5-11," *TTZ* 61 (1952): 186-92.

0700 A. Rolla, "Il passo Cristologico di Filipp. 2,5-11," *ScC* 80 (1952): 127-34.

0701 Lewis A. Curtis, "An Investigation of the Philippians Problem," doctoral dissertation, New Orleans Baptist Theological Seminary, New Orleans LA, 1953.

0702 H. Lattanzi, "Cristo nella gerarchia degli esseri secondo le Lettere della cattività e quelle ai Romani," *Div* 2 (1958): 472-85.

0703 G. Bornkamm, "Zum Verständnis des Christus-Hymnus Phil 2,611," in *Studien zu Antike und Urchristentum: Gesammelte Aufsätze.* Múnich: Kaiser. 1959. Pp. 177-87.

0704   P. Dacquino, "Il testo cristologico di Fil. 2,6-11," *RivBib* 7 (1959): 221-29.

0705   L. Krinetzki, "Der Einfluss von Is 52,13-53,12 Par auf Phil 2,6-11," *TQ* 139 (1959): 157-93, 291-336.

0706   Charles M. Horne, "Let This Mind Be in You," *JETS* 3 (1960): 37-44.

0707   André Feuillet, "L'hymne christologique de l'Epitre aux Philippiens 2:6-11," *RB* 72 (1965): 352-80; 481-507.

0708   John Harvey, "New Look at the Christ Hymn in Philippians 2:6-11," *ET* 76 (1965): 337-39.

0709   L. Krinetzki, "Le serviteur de Dieu," *AsSeign* 37 (1965): 37-45.

0710   Andrew John Bandsta, "Adam and the Servant in Philippians 2:5ff," *CTJ* 1 (1966): 213-16.

0711   Jospeh Coppens, "Les affinités littéraires de l'hymne christologique Phil. 2,6-11," *ETL* 42 (1966): 238-41.

0712   M. Dhainaut, "Les abaissements volontaires du Christ: Philippiens 2,6-11," *BVC* 71 (1966): 44-57.

0713   David H. Wallace, "Note on Morphe," *TZ* 22 (1966): 19-25.

0714   Joseph Coppens, "Une nouvelle structuration de l'hymne christologique de l'épître aux Philippiens," *ETL* 43 (1967): 197-202.

0715   Norman K. Bakken, "New Humanity: Christ and the Modern Age," *Int* 22 (1968): 71-82.

0716   André Feuillet, "L'épître aux Philippiens: hymne christologique," *AmCl* 80 (1970): 733-41.

0717   K. Gamber, "Der Christus-Hymnus im Philipperbrief in liturgiegeschichtlicher Sicht," *Bib* 51 (1970): 369-76.

0718   S. De Ausejo, "Es un himno a Cristo el prólogo de San Juan? Los himnos cristologicos de la Iglesia primitiva y el prólogo del IV Evangelio," in *La escatologia individual neotestamentana* a la luz de las ideas en los tiempos apostolicos. Madrid: Consejo Superior de Investigaciones Científicas, 1972. Pp. 307-96.

0719 Pierre Grelot, "Deux expressions difficiles de Philippiens 2:6-7," *Bib* 53 (1972): 495-507.

0720 Bruno Corsani, "Gesù Cristo è il Signore," in Maria Vingiani, et al., eds., *Ecumenismo oggi: bilancio e prospettive: atti della XIII Sessione di formaziona ecumenica.* Turin: Elle Di Ci, 1975. Pp. 195-205.

0721 B. Eckman, "A Quantitative Metrical Analysis of the Philippians Hymn," *NTS* 26 (1980): 258-66.

0722 H. W. Bartsch, "Der Christushymnus Phil. 2,6-11 und der historische Jesus," *StudE* 7 (1982): 21-30.

0723 J.-C. Basset, "Théologie de la croix et culture indienne. L'interprétation de V. Chakkarai à la lumière de Philippiens 2:6-11," *RHPR* 63 (1983): 417-34.

0724 Hans Becker and Reiner Kaczynski, eds., *Liturgie und Dichtung: Ein interdisziplinäres Kompendium, I: Historische Präsentation.* Sankt Ottilien: EOS Verlag, 1983.

0725 Norman K. Bakken, "Uma nova criaçao: o Cristo para o nosso tempo," *EstT* 24 (1984): 118-28.

0726 Byung-Mu Ahn, "The Body of Jesus-Event Tradition," *EAJT* 3 (1985): 293-309.

0727 Antonio M. Artola, "La mística cristopática de San Pablo de la Cruz," *EE* 60 (1985): 135-56.

0728 William S. Kurz, "Kenotic Imitation of Paul and of Christ in Philippians 2 and 3," in Fernando F. Segovia, ed., *Discipleship in the New Testament.* Philadelphia: Fortress Press, 1985. Pp. 103-26.

0729 Jean Marc Laporte, "Kenosis and koinonia: The Path Ahead for Anglican-Roman Catholic Dialogue," *OC* 21 (1985): 102-20.

0730 Stephen W. Sykes, "The Strange Persistence of Kenotic Christology," in Alistair Kee and Eugene T. Long, eds., *Being and Truth* (festschrift for John Macquarrie). London: SCM Press, 1986. Pp. 349-75.

0731 Albert Verwillghen, "Le Christ Jésus, source de l'humilité chrétienn (Phil 2,6-8)," in Anne-Marie La Bonnardière, ed., *Saint Augustin et la Bible*. Paris: Editions Beauchesne, 1986. Pp. 427-37.

0732 David A. Black, "The Authorship of Philippians 2:6-11: Some Literary-Critical Observations," *CTR* 2 (1988): 269-89.

0733 Jan Botha, "Die Kolossense-himne (Kol 1:15-20)," *HTS* suppl 1 (1989): 54-82.

0734 Sheila Briggs, "Can an Enslaved God Liberate? Hermeneutical Reflections on Philippians 2:6-11," *Semeia* 47 (1989): 137-53.

0735 Alan Neely, "Mission as kenosis: Implications for Our Times," *PSB* N.S. 10 (1989): 202-23.

0736 Roselyne Dupont-Roc, "De l'hymne christologique à une vie de koinonia: Etude sur la lettre aux Philippiens," *EB* 49 (1991): 451-72.

0737 C. Basevi and Juan Chapa, "Philippians 2:6-11: The Rhetorical Function of a Pauline 'Hymn'," in Stanley E. Porter, and Thomas H. lbricht, eds., *Rhetoric and the New Testament*. Sheffield UK: JSOT Press, 1993. Pp. 338-56.

0738 Roland Bergmeier, "Weihnachten mit und ohne Glanz: Notizen zu Johannesprolog und Philipperhymnus," *ZNW* 85 (1994): 47-68.

0739 Gerald Bostock, "Origen's Exegesis of the Kenosis Hymn," in Gilles Dorival and Alain Le Boulluec, eds., *Origeniana sexta: Origène et la Bible*. Louvain: Peeters, 1995. Pp. 531-47.

0740 H. Navarro Cuervo, "La kénosis de Cristo," *May* 22 (1996): 339-436.

0741 S. A. Deane, "Obedience and Humility of the Second Adam: Philippians 2:6-11," *JRR* 1 (1997): 4-12.

0742 S. Wood, "Is Philippians 2:5-11 Incompatible with Feminist Concerns?" *PEcc* 6 (1997): 172-83.

0743   C. Basevi, "Estudio literario y teológico del himno cristológico de la
       epístola a los Filipenses (Phil 2,6-11)," *ScripT* 30 (1998): 439-72.

kerygma
0744   Byung-Mu Ahn, "The Body of Jesus-Event Tradition," *EAJT* 3
       (1985): 293-309.

kingdom of God
0745   Franz Mussner, "Das Reich Christi: Bemerkungen zur Eschatologie
       des Corpus Paulinum," in Michael Böhnke and Hanspeter Heinz, eds.,
       *Im Gespräch mit dem dreieinen Gott: Elemente einer trinitarischen
       Theologie* (festschrift for Wilhelm Breuning). Düsseldorf: Patmos
       Verlag, 1985. Pp. 141-55.

law and gospel
0746   Robert H. Gundry, "Grace, Works, and Staying Saved in Paul," *Bib*
       66 (1985): 1-38.

0747   François Refoulé, "Note sur Romains 9:30-33," *RB* 92 (1985):
       161-86.

0748   Thomas R. Schreiner, "Paul and Perfect Obedience to the Law: An
       Evaluation of the View of E. P. Sanders," *WTJ* 47 (1985): 245-78.

0749   Heikki Räisänen, "Paul's Conversion and the Development of His
       View of the Law," *NTS* 33 (1987): 404-19.

literary criticism
0750   Joseph Coppens, "Les affinités littéraires de l'hymne christologique
       Phil 2, 6-11," *ETL* 42 (1966): 238-41.
Lord's Supper
0751   Luis F. Landaria, "Eucaristía y escatología," *EE* 59 (1984): 211-16.

0752   David G. Peterson, "Further Reflections on Worship in the New
       Testament," *RTR* 44 (1985): 34-41.

mercy
0753   Albert Verwillghen, "Le Christ Jésus, source de l'humilité chrétienn
       (Phil 2,6-8)," in Anne-Marie La Bonnardière, ed., *Saint Augustin et
       la Bible*. Paris: Editions Beauchesne, 1986. Pp. 427-37.

missions
0754   Mark R. Shaw, "Is There Salvation outside the Christian Faith," *EAJT* 2 (1983): 42-62.

0755   Geevarghese Osthathios, "Conviction of Truth and Tolerance of Love," *IRM* 74 (1985): 490-96.

0756   John T. Greene, "Paul's Hermeneutic Versus Its Competitors," *JRT* 42 (1985): 7-21.

0757   Ramón Trevijano Etchverria, "La mision en Tesalonica," *Salm* 32 (1985): 263-91.

0758   Alan Neely, "Mission as kenosis: Implications for Our Times," *PSB* N.S. 10 (1989): 202-23.

Nag Hammadi
0759   Gedaliahu A. G. Stroumsa, "Form(s) of God: Some Notes on Metatron and Christ," *HTR* 76 (1983): 269-88.

obedience
0760   John G. Strelan, "Who Heals the Healers," *Point* 10 (1981): 170-79.

0761   Marcel Doucet, "La volonté humaine du Christ, spécialement en son agonie: Maxime le Confesseur, interprète de l'Ecriture," *ScE* 37 (1985): 123-59.

opponents
0762   R. Jewett, "Conflicting Movements in the Early Church as Reflected in Philippians," *NovT* 12 (1970): 362-90.

0763   H. W. Bateman, "Were the Opponents at Philippi Necessarily Jewish," *BSac* 155 (1998): 39-61.

paraenesis
0764   William S. Kurz, "Kenotic Imitation of Paul and of Christ in Philippians 2 and 3," in Fernando F. Segovia, ed., *Discipleship in the New Testament*. Philadelphia: Fortress Press, 1985. Pp. 103-26.

0765   Derek Thomas, "Standing Firm! Philippians 4:1," *Evangel* 11 (1993): 39-43.

passion
0766 Antonio M. Artola, "La mística cristopática de San Pablo de la Cruz," *EE* 60 (1985): 135-56.

0767 Marcel Doucet, "La volonté humaine du Christ, spécialement en son agonie: Maxime le Confesseur, interprète de l'Ecriture," *ScE* 37 (1985): 123-59.

peace
0768 Carl Loeliger, "Biblical Concepts of Salvation," *Point* 6 (1977): 134-45.

0769 Will K. Morris, "Rejoice Always," *ChrM* 16 (1985): 24.

person and work of Christ
0770 Ralph M. Smith, "An Inquiry into the Nature of the Person and Work of Christ as Revealed in the Imprisonment Epistles," doctoral dissertation, Southwestern Baptist Theological Seminary, Fort Worth TX, 1960.

Philippi, Church at
0771 Alton W. Greenlaw, "Some Factors Contributing to the Distinctiveness of the Philippian Church," doctoral dissertation, Southern Baptist Theological Seminary, Louisville KY, 1949.

prayer
0772 Peter T. O'Brien, "Divine Provision for Our Needs: Assurances from Philippians 4," *RTR* 50 (1991): 21-29.

Rabbinic literature
0773 Mark A. Seifrid, "Paul's Approach to the Old Testament in Romans 10:6-8," *TriJ* N.S. 6 (1985): 3-37.

redaction criticism
0774 David E. Garland, "The Composition and Unity of Philippians: Some Neglected Literary Factors," *NovT* 27 (1985): 141-73.

0775 William O. Walker, "Acts and the Pauline Corpus Reconsidered," *JSNT* 24 (1985): 3-23.

redemption
0776 John G. Gibbs, "Relation between Creation and Redemption according to Philippians 2:5-11," *NovT* 12 (1970): 270-83.

regeneration
0777   John S. Pobee, "Human Transformation: A Biblical View," *MS* 2 (1985): 5-9.

relation to the Old Testament
0778   Joseph Coppens, "Les affinités littéraires de l'hymne christologique Phil 2, 6-11," *ETL* 42 (1966): 238-41.

0779   P. Richardson, "Philippians: The Beginning of the Transpositions," in *Israel in the Apostolic Church*. SNTS #10. Cambridge: University Press, 1969. Pp. 111-17.

0780   Wolfgang Schrage, "Israel nach dem Fleisch," in Hans-Georg Geyer, et al., eds., *"Wenn nicht jetzt, wann dann"* (festschrift for Hans-Joachim Kraus). Neukirchen-Vluyn: Neukirchener Verlag, 1983. Pp. 143-51.

0781   J. Duncan M. Derrett, "Running in Paul: The Midrashic Potential of Hab 2:2," *Bib* 66 (1985): 560-67.

0782   Mark A. Seifrid, "Paul's Approach to the Old Testament in Romans 10:6-8," *TriJ* N.S. 6 (1985): 3-37.

0783   Allan Chapple, " 'The Lord Is Near'," in David Peterson John Pryor, eds., *In the Fullness of Time* (festschrift for Donald Robinson). Homebush West NSW: Lancer, 1992. Pp. 149-65.

0784   Kenneth E. Bailey, " 'Inverted Parallelisms' and 'Encased Parables' in Isaiah and Their Significance for Old and New Testament Translation and Interpretation," in L. J. de Regt, et al., eds., *Literary Structure and Rhetorical Strategies in the Hebrew Bible*. Winona Lake IN: Eisenbrauns, 1996. Pp. 14-30.

0785   S. A. Deane, "Obedience and Humility of the Second Adam: Philippians 2:6-11," *JRR* 1 (1997): 4-12.

0786   P. A. Holloway, *"Bona Cogitarea*: An Epicurean Consolation in Philippians 4:8-9," *HTR* 91 (1998): 89-96.

repentance
0787   Michael B. Dick, "Conversion in the Bible," in Robert D. Duggan, ed., *Conversion and the Catechumenate*. Ramsey NJ: Paulist Press, 1984. Pp. 43-63.

resurrection
 0788   D. M. Stanley, "Christ's Resurrection: A Force in the Christian Life.
        Phil. 3, 10-11)," in *Christ's Resurrection in Pauline Soteriology*.
        Rome: Pontifical Biblical Institute, 1961. Pp. 102-105.

 0789   Ben F. Meyer, "Did Paul's View of the \\surrection of the Dead
        undergo Development?" *TS* 47 (1986): 363-87.

 0790   Joseph A. Fitzmyer, "To Know Him and the Power of His
        Resurrection (Philippians 3:10)," in A.-L. Descamps and André
        Halleux, eds., *Mélanges bibliques en hommage au R. P. Béda Rigaux*.
        Gembloux: Duculot, 1970. Pp. 411-25.

 0791   Anthony Hoekema, "Heaven: Not Just an Eternal Day off," *CT* 29
        (1985): 18-19.

 0792   Ulrich Luck, "Die Bekehrung des Paulus und das paulinische
        Evangelium: zur Frage der Evidenz in Botschaft und Theologie des
        Apostels," *ZNW* 76 (1985): 187-208.

 0793   Richard D. Patterson, "Attaining to the Resurrection," *FundJ* 4
        (1985): 53.

 0794   Jean Doignon, "Comment Hilaire de Poitiers a-t-il lu et compris le
        verset de Paul, Philippiens 3:21?" *VC* 43 (1989): 127-37.

 0795   Randall E. Otto, " 'If Possible I May Attain the Resurrection from the
        Dead'," *CBQ* 57 (1995): 324-40.

rhetoric
 0796   Gerald W. Peterman, "Thankless Thanks: The Epistolary Social
        Convention in Philippians 4:10-20," *TynB* 42 (1991): 261-70.

 0797   Steven J. Kraftchick, "A Necessary Detour: Paul's Metaphorical
        Understanding of the Philippian Hymn," *HBT* 15 (1993): 1-37.

 0798   Samuel Vollenweider, "Die Waagschalen von Leben und Tod: Zum
        antiken Hintergrund von Phil 1,21-26," *ZNW* 85 (1994): 93-115.

 0799   James L. Jaquette, "Life and Death, Adiaphora, and Paul's Rhetorical
        Strategies," *NovT* 38 (1996): 30-54.

0800 Stanley E. Porter and Thomas H. Olbricht, eds., *The Rhetorical Analysis of Scripture: Essays from the 1995 London Conference.* Sheffield: Sheffield Academic Press, 1997.

0801 Jeffrey T. Reed, *A Discourse Analysis of Philippians: Method and Rhetoric in the Debate over Literary Integrity.* Sheffield: Sheffield Academic Press, 1997.

0802 Cynthia B. Kittredge, *Community and Authority: The Rhetoric of Obedience in the Pauline Tradition.* Harrisburg PA: Trinity Press International, 1998.

righteousness

0803 Ulrich Luck, "Die Bekehrung des Paulus und das paulinische Evangelium: zur Frage der Evidenz in Botschaft und Theologie des Apostels," *ZNW* 76 (1985): 187-208.

0804 Marion L. Soards, "The Righteousness of God in the Writings of the Apostle Paul," *BTB* 15 (1985): 104-109.

Roman law

0805 Rodney R. Reeves, "To Be or Not to Be? That Is not the Question: Paul's Choice in Philippians 1:22," *PRS* 19 (1992): 273-89.

sanctification

0806 R. C. Sproul, "Heresies of Holiness," *CT* 30 (1965): 30-31.

0807 Anthony Hoekema, "How We See Ourselves," *CT* 29 (1985): 36-38.

0808 Anthony Hoekema, "Created Persons," *RJ* 36 (1986): 8-11.

0809 Michael Parsons, "Being Precedes Act: Indicative and Imperative in Paul's Writing," *EQ* 60 (1988): 99-127.

sin

0810 Anthony Hoekema, "Created Persons," *RJ* 36 (1986): 8-11.

slavery

0811 Peter Lampe, "Iunia-Iunias: Sklavenherkunft im Kreise der vorpaulischen Apostel (Röm 16:7)," *ZNW* 76 (1985): 132-34.

sociology
> 0812   Marlis Giele, "Zur Interpretation der paulinischen Formel He kat'
>   oikon ekklesia," *ZNW* 77 (1986): 109-25.

> 0813   Jürgen Becker, "Paulus und seine Gemeinden," in Jürgen Becker, et
>   al., eds., *Die Anfänge des Christentums: alte Welt und neue
>   Hoffnung.* Stuttgart: W. Kohlhammer, 1987. Pp. 102-59.

> 0814   Robert A. Wortham, "Christology as Community: Identity in the
>   Philippians Hymn--The Philippians Hymn as Social Drama," *PRS* 23
>   (1996): 269-87.

soteriology
> 0815   D. M. Stanley, "The Christian Eschatological Hope of Salvation. Phil.
>   3, 20-21)," in *Christ's Resurrection in Pauline Soteriology.* Rome:
>   Pontifical Biblical Institute, 1961. Pp. 105-107.

> 0816   Carl Loeliger, "Biblical Concepts of Salvation," *Point* 6 (1977):
>   134-45.

> 0817   David L. Balas, "The Meaning of the 'Cross'," in Andreas Spira and
>   Christoph Klock, eds., *The Easter Sermons of Gregory of Nyssa:
>   Translation and Commentary.* Cambridge: Philadelphia Patristic
>   Foundation, 1981. Pp. 305-18.

> 0818   Peter von der Osten-Sacken, "Heil für die Juden - auch ohne," in
>   Hans-Georg Geyer, et al., eds., *"Wenn nicht jetzt, wann dann"*
>   (festschrift for Hans-Joachim Kraus). Neukirchen-Vluyn:
>   Neukirchener Verlag, 1983. Pp. 169-82.

> 0819   Mark R. Shaw, "Is There Salvation outside the Christian Faith," *EAJT*
>   2 (1983): 42-62.

> 0820   Alvin L. Baker, "Eternal Security Rightly Understood," *FundJ* 3
>   (1984): 18-20.

> 0821   Michael R. Austin, "Salvation and the Divinity of Jesus," *ET* 96
>   (1985): 271-75.

> 0822   Pierre Bonnard, "Conversation biblique avec Jean Delumeau," *FV* 84
>   (1985): 77-81.

0823 Paul Gilbert, "La christologie sotériologique de Kant," *Greg* 66 (1985): 491-515.

0824 Robert H. Gundry, "Grace, Works, and Staying Saved in Paul," *Bib* 66 (1985): 1-38.

0825 John S. Pobee, "Human Transformation: A Biblical View," *MS* 2 (1985): 5-9.

0826 François Refoulé, "Note sur Romains 9:30-33," *RB* 92 (1985): 161-86.

0827 Charles R. Smith, "The Book of Life," *GTJ* 6 (1985): 219-30.

0828 John B. Webster, "Christology, Imitability and Ethics," *SJT* 39 (1986): 309-26.

0829 John B. Webster, "The Imitation of Christ," *TynB* 37 (1986): 95-120.

0830 Heikki Räisänen, "Paul's Conversion and the Development of His View of the Law," *NTS* 33 (1987): 404-19.

0831 Michael Wolter, "Der Apostel und seine Gemeinden als Teilhaber am Leidensgeschick Jesu Christi: Beobachtungen zur paulinischen Leidenstheologie," *NTS* 36 (1990): 535-57.

0832 Per Bilde, "Eskatologi, soteriologi og kosmologi hos Paulus på grundlag af Fil.3,20-21 og beslægtede tekster: Et bidrag til debatten om Gronbechs Paulus-bog," *DTT* 54 (1991): 209-27.

0833 Beat Weber, "Philipper 2,12-13: Text - Kontext - Intertext," *BibN* 85 (1996): 31-37.

suffering
0834 Anne Hetzel, "L'accompagnement des mourants," *FV* 84 (1985): 29-45.

textual criticism
0835 R. Roberts, "Old Texts in Modern Translations: Philippians 1:27," *ET* 49 (1937-1938): 325-28.

0836 Walter M. Nickelson, "A Textual and Manuscript Comparison of Philippians," master's thesis, Midwestern Baptist Theological Seminary, Kansas City KN, 1957.

0837 Charles M. Horne, "Let This Mind Be in You," *JETS* 3 (1960): 37-44.

0838 W. J. Dalton, "The Integrity of Philippians, *Bib* 60 (1979): 97-102.

0839 R. McL. Wilson, "Philippians in Fayyumic," in E. Best and R. McL. Wilson, eds., *Text and Interpretation* (festschrift for Matthew Black). Cambridge: University Press, 1979. Pp. 245-50.

0840 Joseph A. Fitzmyer, "The Aramaic Background of Philippians 2:6-11," *CBQ* 50 (1988): 470-83.

0841 Siegbert Uhlig, "Textcritical Questions of the Ethiopic New Bible," in Alan S. Kaye, ed., *Semitic Studies* (festschrift for Wolf Leslau). Wiesbaden: Otto Harrassowitz, 1991. Pp. 1583-1600.

unity
0842 Robert P. Taylor, "Paul's Doctrine of Unity in the Imprisonment Epistles," doctoral dissertation, Southwestern Baptist Theological Seminary, Fort Worth TX, 1939.

virgin birth
0843 Robert Gromacki, "The Virgin Birth," *FundJ* 1 (1982): 17-19.

wealth
0844 William R. Herzog, "The New Testament and the Question of Racial Injustice," *ABQ* 5 (1986): 12-32.

women
0845 Jean Marc Laporte, "Kenosis and koinonia: The Path Ahead for Anglican-Roman Catholic Dialogue," *OC* 21 (1985): 102-20.

0846 Francis X. Malinowski, "The Brave Women of Philippi," *BTB* 15 (1985): 60-64.

0847 Wendy Cotter, "Women's Authority Roles in Paul's Churches: Countercultural or Conventional?" *NovT* 36 (1994): 350-72.

0848 S. Wood, "Is Philippians 2:5-11 Incompatible with Feminist Concerns?" *PEcc* 6 (1997): 172-83.

word studies

0849 Claude Tassin, "L'apostolat, un 'Sacrifice'? Judaïsme et métaphore paulinienne," in Marcel Neusch, ed., *Le sacrifice dans les religions.* Pp. 85-116.

0850 H. Kruse, "ἁρπαγμός," *VD* 27 (1949): 355-60.

0851 L. Bouyer, "Arpagmos," in *Mélanges Jules Lebreton, RechSR* 39 (1951): 281-88.

0852 H. Kruse, "Iterum 'ἁρπαγμός'," *VD* 29 (1951): 206-14.

0853 R. R. Brewer, "The Meaning of *politeuesthe* in Philippians 1:27," *JBL* 73 (1954): 76-83.

0854 L. Morris, "Kai apaks kai dis," *NovT* 1 (1956): 205-208.

0855 Ceslaus Spicq, "ἐπιποθεῖν désirer ou chérir?" *RB* 64 (1957): 184-95.

0856 J. M. Furness, "Arpagmos eauton ekenōse," *ET* 69 (1957-1958): 93-94.

0857 Donald L. Norbie, "If by Any Means," *EQ* 32 (1960): 224-26.

0858 D. M. Stanley, "A Palestinian Soteriological Theme: Christ as 'Ebed Yahweh. Phil. 2, 6 11)," in *Christ's Resurrection in Pauline Soteriology*. Rome: Pontifical Biblical Institute, 1961. Pp. 95-102.

0859 Joachim Jeremias, "Zu Phil 2:7: Heauton ekenosen," *NovT* 6 (1963): 182-88.

0860 F. E. Vokes, "Arpagmos in Philippians 2:5-11," *StudE* 2 (1964): 670-75.

0861 André Feuillet, "L'hymne christologique de l'Epitre aux Philippiens 2:6-11," *RB* 72 (1965): 352-80.

0862 S. K. Finlayson, "Lights, Stars or Beacons," *ET* 77 (1966): 181.

0863 David H. Wallace, "Note on Morphe," *TZ* 22 (1966): 19-25.

0864 G. D. Kilpatrick, "Blepete: Philippians 3,2," in M. Black and G. Fohrer, eds., *In Memoriam Paul Kahle* (festschrift for Paul Kahle). Berlin: Töpelmann, 1968. Pp. 146-48.

0865 H. R. Moehring, "Some Remarks on sarks in Philippians 3:3," *StudE* 4 (1968): 432-36.

0866 Norbert Baumert, "1st Philipper 4:10 richtig übersetzt?" *BZ* N.S. 13 (1969): 256-62.

0867 Paul C. Böttger, "Die eschatologische Existenz der Christen: Erwägungen zu Philipper 3:20," *ZNW* 60 (1969): 244-63.

0868 John G. Gibbs, "Relation between Creation and Redemption according to Philippians 2:5-11," *NovT* 12 (1970): 270-83.

0869 Ulrich Browarzik, "Die dogmatische Frage nach der Göttlichkeit Jesu," *NZSTR* 13 (1971): 164-75.

0870 Roy W. Hoover, "ἁρπαγμός Enigma: A Philological Solution," *HTR* 64 (1971): 95-119.

0871 Pierre Grelot, "Deux expressions difficiles de Philippiens 2:6-7," *Bib* 53 (1972): 495-507.

0872 Ceslaus Spicq, "Note sur morphe dans les papyrus et quelques inscriptions," *RB* 80 (1973): 37-45.

0873 Thomas F. Glasson, "Two notes on the Philippians hymn 2:6-11," *NTS* 21 (1974): 133-39.

0874 A. Spreafico, "Theos/anthrōpos: Fil. 2,6-11," *RBib* 28 (1980): 407-15.

0875 Leopold Sabourin, "Koinonia in the New Testament," *RSB* 1 (1981): 109-15.

0876 E. C. Miller, "Politeuesthe in Philippians 1:27: Some Philological and Thematic Observations," *JSNT* 15 (1982): 86-96.

0877 Richard D. Patterson, "Pouring out," *FundJ* 2 (1983): 19.

0878 Gedaliahu A. G. Stroumsa, "Form(s) of God: Some Notes on Metatron and Christ," *HTR* 76 (1983): 269-88.

0879 J. Duncan M. Derrett, "Running in Paul: The Midrashic Potential of Hab 2:2," *Bib* 66 (1985): 560-67.

0880 Rolf Gögler, "Inkarnationsglaube und Bibeltheologie bei Origenes," *TQ* 165 (1985): 82-94.

0881 Günter Klein, "Aspekte ewigen Lebens im Neuen Testament: ein theologischer Annähungsversuch," *ZTK* 82 (1985): 48-70.

0882 George W. Knight, "Two Offices and Two Orders of Elders: A New Testament Study," *Pres* 11 (1985): 1-12.

0883 Jean Marc Laporte, "Kenosis and koinonia: The Path Ahead for Anglican-Roman Catholic Dialogue," *OC* 21 (1985): 102-20.

0884 Francis X. Malinowski, "The Brave Women of Philippi," *BTB* 15 (1985): 60-64.

0885 Geevarghese Osthathios, "Conviction of Truth and Tolerance of Love," *IRM* 74 (1985): 490-96.

0886 Richard D. Patterson, "Attaining to the Resurrection," *FundJ* 4 (1985): 53.

0887 Richard D. Patterson, "Laboring for Christ," *FundJ* 4 (1985): 67.

0888 Richard D. Patterson, "The Service of Faith," *FundJ* 4 (1985): 50.

0889 Mark A. Seifrid, "Paul's Approach to the Old Testament in Romans 10:6-8," *TriJ* N.S. 6 (1985): 3-37.

0890 Marion L. Soards, "The Righteousness of God in the Writings of the Apostle Paul," *BTB* 15 (1985): 104-109.

0891 Daniel B. Wallace, "The Semantics and Exegetical Significance of the Object-Complement Construction in the New Testament," *GTJ* 6 (1985): 91-112.

0892 Marlis Giele, "Zur Interpretation der paulinischen Formel He kat' oikon ekklesia," *ZNW* 77 (1986): 109-25.

0893   L. D. Hurst, "Re-enter the Pre-existent Christ in Philippians 2:5-11,"
           NTS 32 (1986): 449-57.

0894   Florence M. Gillman, "Another Look at Romans 8:3: 'In the Likeness
           of Sinful Flesh'," *CBQ* 49 (1987): 597-604.

0895   Angelino S. Di Marco, "Koinonia pneumatos (2 Cor 13:13; Flp
           2:1)--pneuma koinonias: circolaità e ambivalenza linguistica e
           filologica," *FilN* 1 (1988): 63-76.

0896   A. Boyd Luter, "Worship as Service: The New Testament Usage of
           latreuo," *CTR* 2 (1988): 335-44.

0897   Otto Merk, "Nachahmung Christi: zu ethischen Perspektiven in der
           paulinischen Theologie," in Helmut Merklein, ed., *Neues Testament
           und Ethik* (festschrift for Rudolf Schnackenburg). Freiburg: Herder,
           1989. Pp. 172-206.

0898   James D. G. Dunn, "Once More, Pistis Christou," *SBLSP* 30 (1991):
           730-44.

0899   James L. Jaquette, "Life and Death, Adiaphora, and Paul's Rhetorical
           Strategies," *NovT* 38 (1996): 30-54.

0900   Abraham J. Malherbe, "Paul's Self-Sufficiency," in John T. Fitzgerald,
           ed., *Friendship, Flattery, and Frankness of Speech: Studies on
           Friendship in the New Testament W/rld.* Leiden: E. J. Brill, 1996. Pp.
           125-39.

0901   Markus Bockmuehl, " 'The Form of God': Variations on a Theme of
           Jewish Mysticism," *JTS* N.S. 48 (1997): 1-23.

0902   D. T. Knapp, "The Self-Humiliation of Jesus Christ and Christ-Like
           Living: A Study of Philippians 2:6-11," *EvJ* 15 (1997): 80-94.

0903   P. A. Holloway, "*Bona Cogitarea*: An Epicurean Consolation in
           Philippians 4:8-9," *HTR* 91 (1998): 89-96.

0904   J. Moiser, "The Meaning of *koilia* in Philippians 3:19," *ET* 108
           (1998): 365-66.

worship
  0905 David G. Peterson, "Further Reflections on Worship in the New
          Testament," *RTR* 44 (1985): 34-41.

PART THREE

Commentaries

0906 Robert Rainy, *The Epistle to the Philippians*. The Expositor's Bible. New York: A.C. Armstrong, 1903.

0907 William Sanday and Alfred Barry, *The Epistles to the Galatians, Ephesians, and Philippians*. New York: Cassell and Company, 1903.

0908 Albert B. Simpson, *Philippians, Colossians, Thessalonians*. New York: Alliance Press, 1903.

0909 J. M. S. Baljon, *Commentaar op den brief van Paulus aan de Filippiers*. Utrecht: J. Van Boekhoven, 1904.

0910 Girolamo Zanchi, *Commentaar op Paulus' Zendbrief aan de Philippensen*. Kampen: Kok, 1906.

0911 Julius Kogel, *Christus der Herr: Erlauterungen zu Philipper 2:5-11*. Gütersloh: C. Bertelsmann, 1908.

0912 John H. Jowett, *The High Calling: Meditations on St. Paul's Letter to the Philippians*. New York: Fleming H. Revell, 1909.

0913 Adolf von Schlatter, *Die Briefe an die Thessalonicher und Philipper*. Stuttgart: Vereinsbuchhandlung, 1910.

0914 Martin Dibelius, *An die Thessalonicher I, II: An die Philipper*. Tübingen: Mohr, 1911.

0915 Joseph Knabenbauer, *Commentarius in S. Pauli apostoli epistolas. IV, Epistolae ad Ephesios ad Philippenses et ad Colossenses*. Parisiis: Sumptibus P. Lethielleux, 1912.

0916 A. T. Robertson, *Paul's Joy in Christ: Studies in Philippians*. New York: Fleming H. Revell, 1917.

0917 Alfred Plummer, *A Commentary on St. Paul's Epistle to the Philippians*. London: R. Scott, 1919.

0918 Paul Ewald, *Der Brief des Paulus an die Philipper*. Kommentar zum Neuen Testament #11. Leipzig: A. Deichert, 1923.

0919 H. C. G. Moule, *The Epistle of Paul the Apostle to the Philippians*. Cambridge Bible for Schools and Colleges. Cambridge: University Press, 1924.

0920   John H. Michael, *The Epistle of Paul to the Philippians*. Garden City NY: Doubleday, Doran, 1929.

0921   Charles R. Erdman, *The Epistle of Paul to the Philippians*. Philadelphia: Westminster Press, 1932.

0922   J. Huby, *Éptres de la captivité*. Paris: Beauchesne, 1935.

0923   Wilhelm Michaelis, *Der Brief des Paulus an die Philipper*. Theologischer Handkommentar zum Neuen Testament #11. Leipzig: Deichert, 1935.

0924   Seakle Greijdanus, *De brief van den apostel Paulus aan de gemeente te Philippi*. Amsterdam: H. A. van Bottenburg, 1937.

0925   Erik Peterson, *Apostel und Zeuge Christi: Auslegung des Philipperbriefes*. Freiburg: Herder, 1941.

0926   Eduard Thurneysen, *Der Brief des Paulus an die Philipper / ausgelegt fur die Gemeinde von Eduard Thurneysen zweite Auflage*. Basel: F. Reinhardt, 1943.

0927   K. Barth, *Erklälung des Philipperbriefes*. Zollikon: Evangelischer Verlag, 1947.

0928   Pierre Bonnard, *L'Épître de Saint Paul aux Philippiens*. Paris: Delachaux & Niestlé, 1950.

0929   Ernst Lohmeyer, *Der Brief an die Philipper*. Göttingen: Vandenhoeck & Ruprecht, 1953.

0930   Jacobus J. Muller, *The Epistle of Paul to the Philippians: The English Text with Introduction, Exposition and Notes*. The New International Commentary on the New Testament. Grand Rapids: Eerdmans, 1955.

0931   Werner de Boor, *Die Briefe des Paulus an die Philipper und an die Kolosser*. Wuppertal: Brockhaus, 1957.

0932   Kenneth Grayston, *The Epistles to the Galatians and to the Philippians*. London: Epworth Press, 1957.

0933   Rupert E. Davies, *A Colony of Heaven: A Commentary on St. Paul's Epistle to the Philippians*. London: Epworth Press, 1958.

0934 Paul S. Rees, *The Adequate Man: Studies in Philippians*. London: Marshall, Morgan & Scott, 1958.

0935 Carroll E. Simcox, *They Met at Philippi: A Devotional Commentary on Philippians*. New York: Oxford University Press, 1958.

0936 F. W. Beare, *A Commentary on the Epistle to the Philippians*. London: Adam & Black, 1959.

0937 P. Benoit, *Les épîtres de saint Paul aux Philippiens, à Philémon, aux Colossiens, aux Éphésiens*. Paris: Cerf, 1959.

0938 Karl Staab and L. Freundorfer, *Die Thessalonicherbriefe. Die Gefangenschaftsbriefe und die Pastoralbriefe*. Regensburg: Friedrich Pustet, 1959.

0939 Gilbert Bouwman, *De brief van Paulus aan de Filippiers, vertaald en uitgelegd*. Roermond: J. J. Romen, 1965.

0940 Hendrik M. Matter, *De brief aan de Philippenzen en de brief aan Philemon*. Kampen: Kok, 1965.

0941 George Johnston, *Ephesians, Philippians, and Philemon*. The Century Bible, new edition. London: Nelson and Sons, 1967.

0942 Joachim Gnilka, *Der Philipperbrief, Auslegung*. Herders theologischer Kommentar zum Neuen Testament #10. Freiburg: Herder, 1968.

0943 A. F. J. Klijn, *De brief van Paulus aan de Filippenzen*. Nijkerk: Callenbach, 1969.

0944 Jürgen Blunck, *Auf Freude programmiert: ein Brief aus dem Gefangnis*. Wuppertal: Aussaat, 1974.

0945 Josef Ernst, *Die Briefe an die Philipper, an Philemon, an die Kolosser, an die Epheser*. Regensburg: Pustet, 1974.

0946 Alphonse Maillot, *Aux Philippiens d'aujourd'hui*. Geneve: Editions Labor et Fides, 1974.

0947 Jürgen Becker, Hans Conzelmann and G. Friedrich, *Die Brief an die Galater, Epheser, Philipper, Kolosser, Thessalonicher und Philemon*. NTD #8. Göttingen: Vandenhoeck & Ruprecht, 1976.

0948 G. B. Caird, *Paul's Letters from Prison: Ephesians, Philippians, Colossians, Philemon.* Oxford: Oxford University Press, 1976.

0949 G. Giavini, *Gioia e libertà in Cristo. Le lettere di San Paolo ai Filippesi e a Filemone.* Commenti al Nuovo Testamento. Torino: Elle Di Ci, 1976.

0950 James L. Houlden, *Paul's Letters from Prison: Philippians, Colossians, Philemon, and Ephesians.* Philadelphia: Westminster Press, 1977.

0951 J.-J. Loh and E. A. Nida, *A Translator's Handbook on Paul's Letter to the Philippians.* Helps for Translators #19. New York: United Bible Societies, 1977.

0952 Gerhard Barth, *Der Brief an die Philipper.* Zürcher Bibelkommentare NT #9. Zürich: Theologischer Verlag, 1979.

0953 Jean-Francois Collange, *The Epistle of Saint Paul to the Philippians.* London: Epworth Press, 1979.

0954 F. Marin, *Evangelio de la Esperanza. Evangelio de la Unidad.* Madrid: Publicacciones de la Universidad Pontificia Comillas, 1979.

0955 Robert J. Dean, *Philippians: Life at Its Best.* Nashville: Broadman Press, 1980.

0956 Robert G. Gromacki, *Stand United in Joy: An Exposition of Philippians.* Grand Rapids: Baker, 1980.

0957 Hans Schlier, *Der Philipperbrief.* Kriterien #54. Einsiedeln: Johannes Verlag, 1980.

0958 Ernest W. Saunders, *1 Thessalonians, 2 Thessalonians, Philippians, Philemon.* Knox Preaching Guides. Atlanta: John Knox, 1981.

0959 H. Veldhuizen, *Blijdschap en kroon: overwegingen bij de brief van Paulus aan de Filippenzen.* Kampen: Kok, 1981.

0960 Marius Victorinus, *Commentarii in epistulas Pauli ad Galatas, ad Philippenses, ad Ephesios. Italian & Latin Commentari alle epistole di Paolo agli Efesini, ai Galati, ai Filippesi.* Torino: Societé editrice internazionale, 1981.

0961 Maxie D. Dunnam, *Galatians, Ephesians, Philippians, Colossians, Philemon.* Waco TX: Word, 1982.

0962 F. F. Bruce, *Philippians.* Good News Commentary. San Francisco: Harper & Row, 1983.

0963 Gerald F. Hawthorne, *Philippians.* Word Biblical Commentary #43. Waco TX: Word Books, 1983.

0964 J. A. Motyer, *The Message of Philippians: Jesus Our Joy.* Bible Speaks Today. Downers Grove IL: Inter-Varsity Press, 1984.

0965 Wolfgang Schenk, *Die Philipperbriefe des Paulus: Kommentar.* Stuttgart: W. Kohlhammer, 1984.

0966 Fred B. Craddock, *Philippians. Interpretation: A Bible Commentary for Teaching and Preaching.* Atlanta: John Knox Press, 1985.

0967 Rudolf Pesch, *Paulus und seine Lieblingsgemeinde: Paulus, neugesehen: drei briefe an die Heiligen von Philippi.* Freiburg: Herder, 1985.

0968 Mary Ann Getty, *Philippians and Philemon.* The New Testament Message #14. Wilmington: Michael Glazier, 1987.

0969 Peter D. Koehne, *Chi Rho Commentary on the Letter to the Philippians.* Adelaide: Lutheran Publishing House, 1987.

0970 Ralph P. Martin, *Philippians.* New Century Bible Commentary. 2nd ed. Grand Rapids: Eerdmans, 1987.

0971 Thomas Marberry, *Galatians through Colossians.* Nashville: Randall House Publications, 1988.

0972 Moises Silva, *Philippians.* The Wycliffe Exegetical Commentary. Chicago: Moody Press, 1988.

0973 Richard R. Melick, *Philippians, Colossians, Philemon.* The New American Commentary #32. Nashville: Broadman Press, 1991.

0974 Peter T. O'Brien, *The Epistle to the Philippians: A Commentary on the Greek Text.* Grand Rapids: Eerdmans, 1991.

0975 J. Harold Greenlee, *An Exegetical Summary of Philippians.* Dallas: Summer Institute of Linguistics, 1992.

0976 I. Howard Marshall, *The Epistle to the Philippians.* Epworth Commentaries. London: Epworth Press, 1992.

0977 Georges Gander, *Les épîtres de Paul aux Colossiens et aux Philippiens: nouveau commentaire d'apres l'arameen, le grec et le latin.* Saint-Legier, Suisse: Editions Contrastes, 1993.

0978 Ulrich B. Muller, *Der Brief des Paulus an die Philipper.* Theologischer Handkommentar zum Neuen Testament #11. Leipzig: Evangelische Verlagsanstalt, 1993.

0979 Anthony L. Ash, *Philippians, Colossians & Philemon.* Joplin MO: College Press, 1994.

0980 Ben Witherington, *Friendship and Finances in Philippi: The Letter of Paul to the Philippians.* The New Testament in Context. Valley Forge PA: Trinity Press International, 1994.

0981 Gordon D. Fee, *Paul's Letter to the Philippians.* The New International Commentary on the New Testament. Grand Rapids: Eerdmans, 1995.

.0982 Frank Thielman, *Philippians.* The NIV Application Commentary. Grand Rapids: Zondervan, 1995.

0983 Markus Bockmuehl, *A Commentary on the Epistle to the Philippians.* 4th ed. Black's New Testament Commentaries. London: A. & C. Black, 1997.

0984 Daniel J. Harrington, *Paul's Prison Letters: Spiritual Commentaries on Paul's Letters to Philemon, the Philippians, and the Colossians.* Hyde Park NY: New City Press, 1997.

0985 Markus Bockmuehl, *The Epistle to the Philippians.* Peabody MA: Hendrickson Publishers, 1998.

0986 Mark J. Edwards, *Galatians, Ephesians, Philippians. Ancient Christian Commentary on Scripture.* New Testament #8. Downers Grove IL: InterVarsity Press, 1999.

Author Index

Jowett, John W. 0912
Kaczynski, Reiner 0621, 0724
Kantzer, Kenneth S. 0463
Karris, Robert J. 0119
Käsemann, Ernst 0086, 0302
Kilpatrick, G. D. 0357, 0864
Kinniburgh, E. B. F., 0188
Kittredge, Cynthia B. 0680, 0802
Klappert, Bertold 0218, 0620
Klein, Günter 0053, 0546, 0566, 0881
Klijn, A. F. J. 0548, 0943
Klug, Eugene F. 0435
Knabenbauer, Joseph 0915
Knapp, D. T. 0136, 0264, 0269, 0902
Knight, George W. 0004, 0544, 0555, 0882
Koehne, Peter D. 0969
Kogel, Julius 0911
Koperski, Veronica 0120
Kossen, Henk B. 0098, 0570
Kraftchick, Steven J. 0259, 0635, 0797
Kreitzer, L. J. 0292
Krentz, Edgar M. 0062
Krinetzki, L. 0170, 0184, 0705, 0709
Kruse, H. 0139, 0140, 0850, 0852
Kurz, William S. 0573, 0728, 0764
La Bonnardière, Anne-Marie 0404
Laconi, M. 0142
Lampe, Peter 0488, 0811
Landaria, Luis F. 0436, 0564, 0751
Laporte, Jean Marc 0235, 0552, 0729, 0845, 0883
Larrañaga, V. 0159, 0695
Larsson, E. 0175
Lattanzi, H. 0167, 0702
Lee, G. M. 0047
Lefebvre, G. 0289
Léon-Dufour, X. 0050
Loeliger, Carl 0450, 0768, 0816
Loh, J.-J. 0951
Lohmeyer, Ernst 0929
Lopez, E. 0402
Losie, L. A. 0134
Luck, Ulrich 0360, 0792, 0803
Lupoeri, E. 0219
Luter, A. Boyd 0363, 0896

MacKay, B. S. 0654
Maillot, Alphonse 0103, 0518, 0946
Malherbe, Abraham J. 0476, 0900
Malinowski, Francis X. 0444, 0846, 0884
Manns, F. 0213
Manson, T. W. 0643
Marberry, Thomas 0971
Marin, F. 0954
Marshall, I. Howard 0090, 0617, 0669, 0976
Martin, Ralph P. 0125, 0143, 0178, 0190, 0541, 0970
Mas, J. 0010, 0020
Matter, Hendrik M. 0940
Mayer, Bernhard 0332, 0556
McClain, A. J. 0129, 0542
McClendon, James W. 0114
Meeks, Wayne A. 0257
Meinertz, M. 0163, 0699
Melick, Richard R. 0973
Merk, Otto 0416, 0525, 0580, 0897
Meyer, Ben F. 0789
Michael, John H. 0920
Michaelis, Wilhelm 0921
Miller, David W. 0005
Miller, E. C. 0068, 0876
Minear, Paul S. 0254
Moehring, H. R. 0361, 0865
Moiser, J. 0420, 0904
Montague, G. T. 0384
Moreno García, Abdón 0079
Morris, Will K. 0046, 0054, 0335, 0459, 0683, 0769
Morris, L. 0480, 0854
Motyer, J. A. 0964
Moule, C. F. D. 0092
Moule, H. C. G. 0919
Müller, Jacobus J. 0930
Müller, Ulrich B. 0246, 0410, 0522, 0630, 0978
Munn, Gene L. 0596
Murphy-O'Connor, Jerome 0212
Murray, G. W. 0064, 0316, 0331, 0333, 0449, 0487

Wiles, G. P.   0011, 0023, 0031, 0344,
     0464
Wilmington, Harold L.   0127
Wilson, R. McL.   0839
Witherington, Ben   0980
Wolff, Christian   0392
Wolter, Michael   0393, 0831
Wood, S.   0124, 0742, 0848

Wortham, Robert A.   0121, 0593, 0814
Wright, N. T.   0107
Wulf, F.   0042, 0285, 0414
Yai-Chow Wong, Teresia   0625, 0240
Young, Francis   0583
Young, J. Terry   0396
Zanchi, Girolamo   0910
Zedda, S.   0280
Zerwick, M.   0340, 0466